Marlena's Journal

Marlena's Journal

TELLING IT LIKE IT IS
IN
"MINNESOTA—NOT SO NICE"

A Documentary

MARLENA FEARING

To order additional copies of this book, contact:
Xlibris Corporation
1-888-795-4274
www.Xlibris.com
Orders@Xlibris.com
53141

CONTENTS

DEDICATION

I am dedicating this documentary in loving memory to my parents Mary Dambowy and Leo Kowalczyk and to my Sister, Salina Marie Deason. God called Salina on her Birthday last October 11, 2007. In her final months I went back to Minnesota to help care for her while still working on my book. When I couldn't find words to describe the horrors that I experienced, Salina would say, "Oh Sis, you can do it. There is no way to make any of this awful stuff sound pretty. It all happened so just tell it like it is."

Okay Salina, Marlena's Journal will "Tell It Like It is". I felt your presence page after page.

To my Parents—I am what I am thanks to you. I'm the embodiment of both of you with a few added quirks of my own that I picked up along the way. You not only gave me life, the skills to survive and the formidable strength that even surprises me at times.

Even though you're just a memory away, I miss you all terribly.

Much Love,
Marlena

ACKNOWLEGEMENT

I owe a debt of gratitude to so many people—Those that had the courage to support and stand by me when it was not a popular and sometimes a dangerous thing to do. Some found events in their lives compromised for supporting me. A very clear example of that is with Theodor Perlinger, a long-time friend of mine who was sued right along with me for no reason other than he was my friend and supported me. He finally had to leave the Country to get away from these "Hate Merchants" so he could find some peace and tranquility. Another long time friend, and attorney, James Doran also faced challenges for defending and supporting me. Mr. Doran, as an attorney worked for the State Attorney General's Office prior to opening his own practice. He represented me during most of the negotiation process in both Hastings and Lake St. Croix Beach. Therefore, he had first hand knowledge of the corruption taking place. When it became evident that as a witness to the fact he may be called upon to testify in my behalf, he withdrew representation to avoid any conflict.

To my family—my sister, my children, my grandchildren, who shall remain name less for fear of more retaliation. They were the ones that stood by me 24/7 and suffered right along with me. I had always been the one that they looked to for financial advise and support. They witnessed first hand how I was beaten up with a sort of "free for all" with scavengers coming at me from all directions—wanting to take a piece of what I had worked for my entire life; and they felt helpless.

To Lu Ann Stoffel, Mayor of Hastings and Dawn Beedle, Mayor of Lake St. Croix Beach, both of these women had the courage to defend and support me when not a popular thing to do politically. They also found events in their lives compromised for supporting me. It's not very often that you encounter anyone in politics that are willing to take a stand and do the right thing. These women did and received threats as well. In an affidavit from Mayor Beedle, she indicated that she was threatened and forced to send a letter to all residences of Lake St. Croix Beach slandering me. I knew what the threat was without her telling me—a personal ordeal. In court Lu Ann Stoffel, Mayor of Hastings also produced a letter threatening her to resign because she supported me. I will be forever grateful to these women who in my opinion showed great personal character and integrity.

To all those residents, particularly Edith Ryan, Kathryn Smith, Terry Diehl and so many others at the St. Croix Villas who supported me even when they saw where the power was and certainly not with me, but rather the City and it's racist planners, Mary Parr and Robert Swenson. They had the courage to come forward with affidavits to state what they witnessed. Many received threats as well for supporting me.

To Dennis Gauthier and Ron Nechodom for everything that they did to try and help me that went beyond the duty of collections. It just wasn't to be when we had such a collaboration of racists and bigots at every level of government. It also didn't help to have incompetent legal representation.

To all my friends who endured listening to this sad, sordid and sickening ordeal, wondering if I had "gone nuts", but still quietly listening and supporting me.

FOREWORD

The heart of this documentary is how, as a Minnesota real estate developer/ builder and marketer, I was forced out of business not only because I am female; but because I defended and refused to discriminate against minorities. Monetarily, I lost millions of dollars because I dared to stand up to local "sexist and racist cities with far reaching tentacles". However, there can be no value placed on my loss of health due to abuses that I suffered as a result of their unlawful conduct. This documentary depicts that there is something rather sinister and corrupt about a government that incarcerates me for upholding the law and rewards my assets to those who broke the law in aiding to destroy my business. But that is exactly what happened as evidence shows.

When I had made the decision to write and publish this documentary I was focused primarily on the discriminatory aspect and the egregious human rights violations taking place in Minnesota. I had no intention of my documentary becoming a portrait of flagrant government corruption with politicians and judges at their disposal feeding that process—but it is what it is and that is where the evidence led me. As I reviewed the documents, it became clear that the majority of the players are Republican. To my Republican friends who take issue with those allegations, I say "please withhold judgment until you have read the book in its entirety." Then I have two questions—1.) Is this the freedom and democracy that our young men and women in uniform are dying to protect? 2.) Are these the kind of people we want controlling and representing our Country? It gives me no pleasure and I feel great sadness and sorrow in exposing this, but how is America to get back on track if what I uncovered is allowed to continue? As an American, I feel it is my duty to take a stand and speak up. Silence and indifference has already fed this travesty far too long. This is not an attack on America, but rather on the "bums" that we have put in office. Politically I am an independent, and I consider myself

11

to be a "Centrist" with a "compassionate heart" who has always championed for human rights. What happened to me is not the American way and I wish that I could just wake up and find this to be a horrible nightmare and it all really didn't happen. Unfortunately thousands upon thousands of court files and other related documents are the reality.

In this documentary, I am naming names and telling it the way it is. These people need to be voted out of office or impeached for their criminal conduct. They've been fed from the public trough much too long for bad behavior at taxpayer's expense. These are politicians that are supposed to be working for the American People. They have a lot of explaining to do for allowing the eradication of our Constitutional Freedoms. The temerity of these people to thumb their noses and allow the kind of sabotage of our Constitution as what I describe in this documentary is unconscionable.

This story is a perfect example of how "We the People" have become "We the servants of a broken government". I have difficulty understanding how America got so turned on its ear? This is not just a story of politics at play even though it is much to do about politics, abuse of judicial power that has dictated much of what has happened to me, but rather a story depicting the incredulous hypocrisy in our government. I was attacked repeatedly for daring to stand up and do the "right thing", legally, morally and ethically. What I have discovered through this process is that for far too many Americans, doing the "right thing" means doing what doesn't cost anything or inconvenience us in any way, so we choose to look on and do nothing. **"The world is a dangerous place not because of those who do evil, but because of those who look on and do nothing"**. (Albert Einstein)

I had everything to lose and nothing to gain financially by standing up and defending what America stands for . . . . "Freedom and Democracy for all its citizens". My story will tell what a price I had to pay for what should be guaranteed to all of us under the U.S. Constitution; a right to earn a living, a right to own property, a right to free speech, a right to equal protection and due judicial process. I had my home, my properties and all my assets taken from me; and I was stripped of my constitutional rights because I refused to deny housing for minorities. This should not be happening in America, but it is as evidence will show. This entire process appeared to be facilitated by Bush's appointed right wing neo-conservative judges and his U.S. Department of Justice.

This documentary is based in Minnesota, however, clearly the trickle down arrogance and abuse of power by the Bush Administration fed the blames of the escalation of abuses transpiring there. This story, like so many other stories out there, is just one more tragic example of how under the Bush Presidency our Constitution was trampled on by Bush and his appointees. Mr. Bush seemed to have all of his bases covered. First the "Rule of Law" was ignored at the U.S. Justice Department (as a criminal matter) and any endeavor to seek justice in the courts (civilly) like minded judicial appointees by Bush refused to hear or see any evidence and summarily dismissed the case. A report by (People for the American Way) PFAW—"Confirmed Judges, Confirmed Fears" by Ralph G. Ness (This report validates my allegations that activist judges nominated to the courts by President Bush and his Republican Congress "Threatens the Rights of ordinary Americans" by legislating from the bench instead of upholding the "Rule of Law").

There used to be a time when we could at least look to the courts for some sort of justice even if the process wasn't exactly perfect. The "Rule of Law" was just that and it meant something. My recent court experiences, however, were anything but lawful. The process reminded me of a Barnum and Bailey "Freakshow" that I once attended as a little girl. I was just as unimpressed then as I am now. Bush's U.S. Justice Department was equally irrelevant in protecting the Constitution and eradicating civil rights abuses.

When I proposed a housing project in one river valley City in Minnesota, they were adamant about not wanting minorities taking up residency. One councilmember stated at a council meeting (Taped) that if the City provided tax increment financing to reduce the rents, it would bring in all the undesirables, "the Blacks, Hispanics, Indians, Welfare and God only knows what all". They were not one bit shy about telling me that "I needed to bring in a man" if I wanted to get the contract. In another river valley City the City's Mayor and a councilmember told me point-blank that minorities—especially Hmong, and African-Americans were not welcome. They also said they preferred a male developer. My African-American buyers were routinely denied building permits. This is not the American way!

In 2000, under the Clinton Administration both HUD and U.S. Justice found both gender and racial discrimination and froze the City's funds pending further action. However, shortly thereafter the Bush

Administration came into power and the file was inexplicably closed. HUD Case # 05-00-0466-8.

Once U.S. Justice closed the file, the City perceived that as a "green light" that they could discriminate with impunity and they retaliated against me for reporting their discriminatory practices. **This move in itself by the Bush Administration showed a blatant disregard for civil rights abuses. This was not a Democratic process, but rather a process of tyranny by using the judicial system as political maneuvering to retaliate against me by taking away my properties.**

One Black family had the misfortune of purchasing a home through a resale, only to find their home taken from them with the help of a judge friendly to City Hall who was appointed by Republican Governor Arne Carlson. **When as President of the Homeowner's Association, I protested their illegal eviction; I was convicted of "meddling with Association affairs" and sentenced to 30 days in jail. The motive was obvious—to take my assets, slander my name, terrorize me; and evict the only black family in town.**

Since the U.S. Justice Department refused to protect our rights under the Constitution, the Black family joined me in a federal lawsuit in Federal District Court in Minneapolis. The judge assigned to our case was a judge appointed by President George W. Bush in 2002. She refused to see or hear any evidence against any government official because to do so would violate their 11th amendment rights. No mention was made however, as to the violation of rights that the African-American family and I suffered by such "arrogant abuse of power." This is not the American way!

Interestingly, of all the federal judges on the bench this same judge was also assigned to another case in which this same City took 1/3 of my land (without compensation) and then forced me to build a public water shed for the community, also at my expense. In that case as well, the judge didn't want to see the evidence and ruled a Summary Judgment in favor of the City. Both of these cases were appealed to the 8th circuit district court. The findings recently came down in both cases and the appellate judges affirmed the judge's decisions. All of the judges on the panel were also judges that made the PFAW report, "Confirmed Judges—Confirmed Fears" as judges appointed by President Bush who have established a record of violating judicial due process laws. (See, e.g. People For the American Way Foundation, http://www.pfaw.org).

The irony in all of this, I had to live in exile due to threats on my life and three of the African-Americans who were evicted for being the "wrong color" are apparently the "right color" to fight a war. They are now serving their country in Afghanistan and Iraq fighting for our supposed "Freedom and Democracy". **"Such a dichotomy, we defend Democracy abroad and retaliate against citizens who attempt to defend it at home."**

INTRODUCTION

This is a true story based on real events that I have documented for the past 15 years with supporting court documents, affidavits, correspondence, taped conversations, and case files which substantiates and supports every allegation that I've made. The sheer blatant and overt manner in which some of these offenses were committed depicts the arrogance of these individuals. The idea that they really believe that somehow they are superior in design, above the law and immune from any prosecution for their corruption shows the narcissistic attitudes of these government officials, including judges.

It's difficult for me to really know where to begin to tell this story as it is so "beyond belief", un-American; and contrary to everything we are taught to believe about our government and society. We're taught that we live in a Democracy and that the rule of law applies to everyone, that we all are created equal in the eyes of the law, that we have a Constitution that would be upheld to give equal protection to everyone and judicial and political tyranny only exists in foreign lands. Based on my experiences with Minnesota government these teachings are a complete fairy tale.

When I refused to participate with a City's efforts to prevent minorities from taking up residency, I was viciously attacked and vilified. Apparently demonizing me would somehow make their conduct less egregious. Clearly, directives were given by the City to two of their City planners, their attorney and others to initiate a terror campaign against me in an attempt to force me out from my project and out of business. They initiated bogus lawsuits, trespassed and destroyed my property. They stalked, harassed and assaulted me and my African-American grandson with a deadly weapon (vehicle) in an attempt to hit us. These are federal crimes of hate, yet local authorities, state authorities and federal authorities refused to file charges or prosecute them for their criminal acts. When I attempted to get a protective order on three separate occasions from the local Washington County courts, I was denied such protection. On my third attempt, I was told if I made any more attempts for a protective order, I would get an order for contempt. I tried to sell my property and simply walk away from this uncivilized behavior, but I was prevented from accomplishing that as well.

By nature, I am a very peaceful and even-tempered individual, but also known to stand my ground and defend my principles regardless of my challenger. I am tolerant, obliging and a reasonable individual who has always looked to resolve any conflict by conciliation rather than confrontation. Perhaps my easy-going nature was perceived as an inability or unwillingness to defend myself. They guessed incorrectly. In any event, I believe that it is my God given right to enjoy the freedoms guaranteed to all of us under the Constitution of this great Country. I made repeated attempts to reach some sort of compromise with this City, but compromise was not in their plans. Compromise doesn't exist under this City's fascist government. They could not take a chance, given my reputation as an equal opportunity housing developer, to allow me the freedom to develop my property. The extreme measures these officials took to keep their City "All White" depicts the racial intolerance that exists even today. This is not the American way!

The City maintained that I gave them my land for a City watershed, I did no such thing. What this City did was nothing short of theft and extortion. They had all the power, while I had none. My choices as I saw it were to either allow myself to become a victim or attempt a victory with the odds greatly stacked against me. I chose the latter and fought back as best I could, until my health started to deteriorate from all the stress caused from this insane behavior by these government officials. Even though the "Rule of Law and evidence was on my side, it made no difference to these criminals. **Thou shalt not be a victim. Thou shalt not be a perpetrator. Above all, thou shalt not be a bystander"**. Holocaust Museum, Washington, D.C.

The corruption in that Minnesota valley has existed for so very long unchallenged and they never expected anybody, especially a woman to stand up to their dirty deeds. Apparently they never encountered a developer who puts people first—especially one who couldn't be bought—became a real challenge for them. The harder I fought to uphold the law and defend the Constitution, the more the establishment locked arms and retaliated against me. The law was supposed to protect me. It did not. The judicial system was supposed to protect me. It did not. The governmental agencies set up to protect against such discrimination should have protected me. They did not. I had several law firms hired to represent and defend me. They did not. I believe they also have a lot of explaining to do for their negligence in this matter. Their gross negligence and incompetence would suggest that somebody got to them with a lot more money than I had. This, to me has all the elements of a Mafia-like organization.

I have never been a believer in conspiracy theories, but this one certainly made me a believer. There is something very much amiss and no explanation for this bizarre behavior by authorities. Because of what happened to me is so unbelievable, I have written much of this documentary through witnesses as the eyes of third parties who *under oath* prepared affidavits and letters as to what they observed and witnessed. How could such a pocket of "lawlessness" exist for so long and continue without prosecution at a federal level since these are federal crimes is simply remarkable?

I don't know what transpires in other States. I can only tell you what I know for sure, and what I experienced in Minnesota government and its judiciary counterpart. Underneath the "Minnesota Nice" façade, I discovered a "Minnesota Not So Nice" government that is sexist, racist, bigoted and corruption is rampant, particularly in the judicial system. **I have evidence to show that we have state sanctioned discrimination, both racial and gender, and improprieties at the state and federal judicial levels. Court documents and my files are available for anyone who wishes to try and prove me wrong.**

I have never marched or protested for any cause. I have *never* challenged authority and I have been around a long time. Even as a supposed "free society" we need authority, law and order; but corrupt authority that violates state and federal laws is quite another thing. The distinction here in this case is "authority conducting themselves as criminals". In Minnesota if you challenge the "unlawful conduct" of those "In Charge", the "Desiders", kind of like what we have in Washington, D.C.; they will destroy you. What I also have discovered is that in Minnesota, we have the written law and then "no law" for all of those with government positions (those that don't have to account for their conduct) including judges, particularly those in Washington County. They write findings which distort or twist the evidence and essentially they write whatever finding they need to fit the occasion or to get a conviction. And if that isn't possible, they just change or destroy the evidence. The end justifies the means for these miniature potentates to keep their power and protect their fiefdoms.

They work like parasites—feeding on a corrupt system. How they operate under the radar away from detection and scrutiny by the public is simply amazing which will be detailed further in this book. The networking is like a complicated tangled mass of wiring that has no beginning or end. To establish who is doing what to or for whom is indistinguishable as I have found. Where did it all start? In Hastings, Minnesota, but without a doubt this outrage manifested to the point of insanity with the City of Lake St. Croix Beach's Mayor John Jansen, a former Washington *County Attorney*, a State Administrative *Law Judge*, and *councilmember*. If anybody should know the law, this man should being an attorney for 50 years, but apparently the "Rule of Law" doesn't apply to him. I was warned by many local residents that he has more power than the Devil and to never challenge him as he is not only mean-spirited, but also a very well connected Republican. It seems that is where the cause and source of the corruption is derived. Yet, he has others do his dirty deeds while he hides in the grass like a snake.

According to President Bush we are fighting terrorism abroad, to that I say, "Excuse me, Mr. President, we are being terrorized right here at home with threats and fear". Given my experience, we as Americans have our own form of terrorism—powerful government officials, trampling on our Constitution and destroying our very basic freedoms and democracy. This includes judges both at state and federal level who are fulfilling a political agenda using "Fear Tactics" rather than following the "Rule of Law".

This is not meant to be a blanket condemnation of all judges. That is not my intent in writing this documentary, but even if only one judge behaves contrary to the "Rule of Law", that is one too many. In spite of what happened to me, *I have the greatest admiration for those judges who work diligently to be fair, honest, follow the "Rule of Law" and uphold the integrity of the judicial system, only to find they have twisted colleagues in their circle who wish to destroy the very backbone of this Nation—trust and fairness in the judicial process.* I was raised to believe that judges are right up there with God, so you can imagine my dismay to find such corruption in the judicial process. There are many good judges, both Republican and Democratic appointed, but unfortunate for me none of the "good judges" (those that rule on the evidence and the law) were assigned to any of my cases. That would have undermined the process for whoever was orchestrating my demise. Evidence will show that the judiciary was used at both the state and federal level to retaliate against me for "Blowing the Whistle" on discrimination and standing up to corrupt government officials. I now know why Governors and Presidents fight to stack the courts with like-minded judges—to carry out their own personal ideological endeavors and to hell with the "Rule of law" or the Constitution.

In some parts of the world, if you challenge the system, you get put to death. In Minnesota "The Establishment" retaliates against you by destroying your business, taking all of your assets and rewarding them to those who participated in the scam. The method and the means are usually justified by third parties who also have an interest at stake, wanting a piece of the pie, or are threatened by authorities to cooperate. So now you have two accomplices swearing to the truth, and if they need a third or a fourth, trust me, they'll find them. Integrity and honesty are rare commodities in Minnesota's governmental process and up for grabs around every corner, so I found. Evidence will show that the legal system was equally culpable. For me, this has been a real "eye opener" as to the backroom politicization of the judicial process.

If you dare to challenge the wrong-doing by authorities by filing a complaint with a supposed regulatory or investigative agency, retaliation is eminent. It seems that a popular method is to simply send the file to another government Agency (clearing house) for a "whitewashing" in the cleansing process. If government is the perpetrator, agencies such as Minnesota Department of Human Rights, Housing and Urban Development too often, "Hear no evil and see no evil". The same is true for the judicial process. At the District court level, evidence is twisted and distorted to achieve the desired result and if necessary, files simply disappear or documents hi-jacked. If you challenge the process to a higher court, chances are the original findings simply get rubberstamped. Rubber-stamped justice was acknowledged by Judge Richard Arnold of the United States Court of Appeals (8th Circuit) in a speech that he gave before the Drake University Law School.

Many have asked me the same question that I have pondered repeatedly myself, "How can this be happening in America, particularly Minnesota—Minnesotans are so nice"? I guess the answer is as long as we as a society allow this to go unchallenged and are willing to tolerate it. We get the government we deserve. Is this the beginning of a scenario that happened before? **"First they came for the Jews. I was silent. I was not a Jew. Then they came for the Communists. I was silent. I was not a Communist. Then they came for the trade unionists. I was silent. I was not a trade unionist. Then they came for me. There was no one left to speak for me".** (Martin Niemoller)

Minnesotans are nice people. I am a Minnesotan and I love Minnesotans. This is a side of Minnesota that is "not so nice" that many don't know about because they trust that the system works. ***But if you push for answers as I did, you will definitely get a visit from the "Boogey Man".*** Most Minnesotans are a trusting people with strong work ethics and a good value system. They nod in politeness and courtesy when those of importance approach, deserving or not. ***It's the government that is corrupt.*** I think the answer to why that is so, is quite simple. We all want to believe that our elected officials and government are doing the right thing to protect our way of life, so we go about our busy daily lives with apathy and unsuspecting of what is taking place behind the scenes.

Bottom line to all of this is, the government (state and federal were equally complicit) in stealing my assets for my refusal to discriminate and violate state and federal housing laws. Where did I get the impression that you go to jail for breaking the law? Not true, in Minnesota you go to jail for trying to uphold the law, at least when it comes to discrimination against minorities. In my naiveté I believed that discrimination was unlawful and that we have agencies in place to prohibit such conduct. Well, let me tell you what I so painfully discovered, that just ain't so in the land of 10,000 lakes and 10,000 government hacks.

"Discrimination, destroying damaging evidence by government officials and judges is perfectly legal and done all the time", according to a source at the U.S. Justice Department in D.C. under the Bush Administration. That was the official reason that I was given for their refusal to prosecute discriminatory conduct by the City and judges equally complicit. In the previous Clinton administration, the U.S. Justice Department froze this city's funds and prosecution was eminent. How can it be that under one administration there is a finding of both racial and gender discrimination sufficient to freeze a City's funds and with a new administration the case is simply closed very quietly with no explanation?

You can't tell me politics doesn't dictate segregation. **What is happening in the St. Croix Valley is State sponsored discrimination. The Minnesota Department of Human Rights knows it, Governor Pawlenty knows it, The Minnesota State Attorney General's Office knows it, Federal Housing and Urban Development knows it, and the U.S. Justice Department knows it; but, nobody seems to give a care. I have written numerous letters of complaint informing all of them as to what is taking place but, to no avail. Every complaint I made, in return I was rewarded with yet another nail in my coffin.**

Once the local authorities discovered that they would not be held accountable by the U.S. Justice Department for their criminal conduct, they unleashed such furor, terror and retaliation against me that would send anyone into exile. I still refused to be silenced or move until I had no choice when *they took my land, my house and threatened my life and that of my Grandson* who was merely a child at the time. **"Once a government is committed to the principle of silencing the voice of opposition, it has only one way to go, and that is down the path of increasingly repressive measures, until it becomes a source of terror to all its citizens and creates a Country where everyone lives in fear".** (Harry Truman)

I've been a Minnesotan all of my life and I never knew that this side existed until I became involved in developing housing which would include housing for minorities. I will also say that Minnesotans as a whole are not racist and bigoted so the question then becomes, how did our government get that way?

When I worked as a real estate consultant and project manager for a development firm in Edina, Minnesota, I traveled the entire State of Minnesota and even into Wisconsin. Not once did I feel any animosity directed towards me as a female developer and never did I hear any City official tell me that they didn't want minorities coming to their community. That is, until I ventured out to the eastern Minnesota valley, from Hastings on up to Stillwater. There is less than .05% minority and now we know why. That has been accomplished by plan and design by local City Government Officials who wish to keep their city's "All White".

I am beginning to believe that there has got to be major pollution in the river water that has caused such warped thinking and craziness amongst these government officials. Of course, they think that I am the crazy and kooky one for daring to stand up to their insanity. And the more insane their behavior becomes, the more unbelievable this story becomes. That's obviously what they are banking on. I believe this time, they broke the bank on believability because the evidence that I have accumulated over a 15 year period to prove my allegations are irrefutable. Talk about stepping into yesterday's mafia-like existence—Cronyism, Corruption, and Cover-up at every level of government. For a moment, I thought I was in Chicago.

AN UNLIKELY REBEL

Marlena Anna Dambowy Kowalczyk was raised on a farm in Northern Minnesota by parents of Polish—Catholic ancestry who taught me that by upholding the law, respecting authority, being honest and with hard work and perseverance I could accomplish anything. I inherited my Mother's determination and strong Constitution; and my Father's tenacity. That combination is the backbone of my survival skills. Both of my parents wore their hearts on their sleeves, had a terrific sense of humor, tolerant of all people, and the cup was always half full. Their teachings worked well for me my entire life and I achieved much success in real estate; that is until I encountered the "Valley of Evil" and I lost all ability to freely use my professional skills that took years to develop. I was blessed with much abundance through perseverance and hard work when I had the free will to exercise my real estate experience without government interference and control.

My greatest achievement however, was in raising my three children and my grandson, Brandon Ray who is the "love of my life". That is not to say that I love my children any less, it's just that Brandon was a special gift to me. He is of African-American and Indian descent. Having Brandon in my life was a Spiritual awakening for me that I cannot explain. My purpose for existence took on a whole new meaning and direction. There is a reason why I was blessed with such a "Special Kid". I believe that when God designed my life, He had a plan and Brandon Ray was very much a part of that plan.

Even though God is very much a part of my every day life, I seldom go to church. That is not because I have anything against organized religion, I just prefer talking to God without a middle man. Too often I saw my tormentors sitting next to me in the same pew proclaiming to be Christians when their deeds were those of the Devil and certainly not Christ. **It seems to me that**

evil-doers are more exacting in their exuberant and joyful wickedness when they do it from a religious conviction.

From what I remember of my childhood, I was petite and frail, but my spirited and strong willed personality compensated for any deficiency in my stature. It is not my nature to look for a fight, but fight I must against racial intolerance and social injustice. Being raised in the "Old School" mentality, would hardly make me a candidate to desire to challenge authority. **I have experienced life in some very tumultuous times. And I have existed for more than a half century, but I have never experienced the kind of corruption that exists in government as today.** Throughout my life I saw much unfairness and injustice and I tried to make changes where I could and what I couldn't change I just ignored, put it on a shelf for another day and walked away like most people do—"live and let live".

Today is a new "Awakening" for me, the day for me to stand up and say, "enough is enough". **This time it is different because the pocket of evil I encountered is so corrupt that I feel challenges our Democracy, our basic civil liberties and who we are as Americans. This is simply not the Democracy and Freedoms that our young men and women are laying down their lives to protect.** I believe that if we are a principled and moral people it is incumbent upon all of us to speak the truth and expose the lies of a government that is destroying our Country. I don't think that is unpatriotic, but rather to the contrary. We, as Americans all have a duty to protect and safeguard our Freedom and Democracy from threats, whether foreign or within. **It seems of late, however, that we incarcerate all the petty crooks, while electing the professional ones to run our Country.**

I have given much of my time and energy to volunteer as an advocate for abused children and women in the capacity of a court appointed Guardian Ad Litem. I champion many causes quietly, without fanfare or tooting my horn for recognition. As an eldest daughter of seven siblings, the role of caretaker came naturally to me, and it is a role I continue to play today. I have always tried to live my life with passion and purpose. **I believe that it is important that all of us make a positive contribution in our society and leave a mark to show that we indeed did exist. For me, none of this has ever been about the money. If it were, I would have sold my soul long ago.**

I have been asked many times, why are you challenging the establishment when you can't win? It is not I who is challenging the establishment; but rather it is the establishment challenging the "Rule of Law" and I happen to stand in their way. The establishment chose to attack and demonize me when I reminded them that their conduct was unlawful. In spite of all that has happened to me, I still believe that America is worth defending and protecting from those who have chosen to attack the very backbone of this Nation—The Constitution and the Judicial Process. The U.S. Constitution is the birthright of all Americans. It's our national treasure.

THE VALLEY OF EVIL

The Tale of two Cities, Hastings and Lake St. Croix Beach

The St. Croix Valley is a beautiful serene and picturesque area. The St. Croix River flows along the banks of Washington and Dakota County in one of the most beautiful settings in the country. Yet just 20 miles from the capital of Minnesota and the seat of justice, there lives a monster that has turned back the clock of the true meaning of Democracy and Freedom and everything this great Country represents. The archaic and uncivilized attitudes and conduct of the establishment is beyond belief. The minority population is less than one percent. The people of Hastings and Lake St. Croix Beach are neither guilty nor apathetic. Most Minnesotans simply are not aware of what is transpiring and then there are those that have lost their wisdom to differentiate between good and evil and aren't about to challenge the establishment in any event. Like most evil this can't be out in the open for everyone to see. If it were, nobody would tolerate it. Yet it exists because nobody has challenged or exposed it.

These two cities were among the first Minnesota cities to come into existence, due to the rivers flowing through them which brought river trade in the early days. However, they seemingly have not updated their "draconian attitudes" relative to slavery and discrimination.

The common thread between these two cities is a fascist existence. How can this be in a supposed Democratic Society? They have no regard for the law, and their regimes are oppressive and unjust. What I found most interesting in working behind the scenes is that the elected City officials are really not the decision makers, but rather the law firms representing them. When I solicited residents in Hastings for feedback regarding what they envisioned for housing, I was repeatedly told that it was the "Mafia on the Hill" that makes those decisions and their input was unimportant. Since I was not a resident of that City, I inquired as to what they meant by that. I was told repeatedly that everyone knows that it is the City Attorney that runs the town because council members always follow the directives of the City Attorney, Shawn Moynihan.

I learned this to be true also in Lake St. Croix Beach. The City Council only voted as instructed by Mayor John Jansen and the City Attorney. And the council itself was hand picked by John Jansen. The reasoning was obvious, to remain in control and if he lost an election, a council member that was voted in simply resigns and Mr. Jansen was brought back in through the back door as the replacement. That's Democracy in Lake St. Croix Beach.

When I attempted to register and vote for a general election in the City of Lake St. Croix Beach, I was told by Linda O'Donnell, City Clerk, that I would have to produce documentation to prove that I was a resident. I produced my passport, driver's license, electric and water bills, and several letters sent to my address. Still that did not suffice for me to vote.

Excerpt from an affidavit of Mayor Dawn Beedle

"I was Mayor at the time that City Clerk, Linda O'Donnell refused to allow Ms. Fearing the right to register and vote".

These two cities shared a trade secret in "How to Successfully Discriminate" under the radar to avoid any detection and avoid legal ramifications. In other words, they found a means which would allow them to discriminate, if they generated a paper trail to sufficiently camouflage their pretext for discrimination. The most obvious one was to prevent a certain class of people from taking up residency through their zoning process. This was true for the City of Hastings as well as the City of Lake St. Croix Beach. By zoning for only residential, in their "twisted thinking" would prevent minority inhabitants from gaining occupancy in their Cities, whom they referred to as the "Undesirables"(as described by a Hastings councilmember) the "Riff-Raff" (as described by Lake St. Croix Beach Mayor, John Jansen).

If multiple housing was to be given a consideration in either City, it would be for senior housing only. The idea being that since the City was 100% Caucasian, only the elderly would eventually need to downsize to an apartment or townhouse and any younger families who couldn't afford a house would be excluded because in theory Caucasians could afford to buy and minorities could only afford to rent. I must admit that I was rather sickened that this kind of rationale existed today.

I discovered that in the City of Hastings, they had a development contract with Mark Ulfers, their County HRA Director (Housing and Redevelopment Authority) whose job was to implement financing for housing through tax credits, tax increment financing and housing revenue bonds. The only problem with the tax credits is that when Congress allocated the tax credits through the State agencies, the HRA director had first pickings. This essentially eliminated a private entity to gain access for those funds and it was up to the HRA to make them available to the private sector or hog them for his agency, which usually ended up to be the latter. The director saw to it that this housing was for senior only so he and the City had a cozy little arrangement that essentially amounted to discrimination by a government authority that is supposed to prevent such discriminatory activity rather than encouraging and arranging for it.

The following will show how these two cities exacted their behavior when negotiating with me.

- They gave erroneous data to council members than what I proposed.
- They created impossible standards and an atmosphere of confusion.
- Restrictive and ambiguous language was drafted in the contracts and then blame laid on me or my legal counsel.
- Missing tapes or altered documents was the norm rather than the exception and so was consistent tampering with the truth to downright lying.
- Obscuring their discriminatory conduct by bringing in third parties (who have a financial interest) i.e. engineers, inspectors, attorneys, etc. to shift the blame and cover up their wrong doings. That's how we ended up with a box car full of documents that are not relevant.
- Creating a paper trail that "Houdini" couldn't untangle.
- Portraying me as unqualified and incompetent, which would automatically give them their, "articulated reasoning to discriminate".
- There appeared to be a circus-like atmosphere with no real serious intent to negotiate with any professionalism or in good faith.

Both cities told me that I needed to "bring in a man" to give me the credibility I needed to get the contract. **I had at that point in time, twenty five years experience in the real estate business and I had both a State**

general contractor's license and a real estate broker's license. I needed nothing more legally to conduct business, yet I was prevented from doing so. In their eyes they viewed me as unqualified to do business in their cities due not only to my gender, but what I represented, "an equal opportunity housing developer". Other male developers didn't have the qualifications that I did in terms of education and licenses. Therefore, my gender was what disqualified me.

Hastings Mayor Stoffel, wrote to the Hastings Gazette and made these comments in reference to my proposed housing project.

"I believe this project met with opposition from the very beginning due to politics and discrimination—discrimination against the developer because she is a woman, and discrimination against Hastings residents because of age, race and income."

Mayor Stoffel also testified in my behalf at the trial, essentially stating that it was her firm belief that my gender was what prevented me from getting the development contract in Hastings. She testified that council members and staff could not get past the fact that "I was a woman and I did not have a hammer in my back pocket". She also testified that she acknowledged telling me that I could not do business in Hastings because I was too attractive and I needed a "Penis". (Dakota County District Court file # C3-96-1884.)

Lake St. Croix Beach Mayor Dawn Beedle made similar comments as follows to my Attorney James Doran and GNA Investigators.

Mayor Beedle acknowledged that Mayor John Jansen had a problem with women and that I would only have credibility in his eyes if I brought in a man. She inquired as to whether my investor was male and if so, for me to bring him to a council meeting to speak for me.

In a meeting at her home, when asked what she perceived to be the problems, Mayor Beedle indicated that Mr. Jansen had difficulty with a smart and attractive woman, particularly one that was organized. She went on to say that he (Jansen) was more used to dealing with men that came in with drawings on a napkin or placemat as opposed to professional drawn renderings as I presented. In Mayor Beedle's opinion, Mr. Jansen saw me as a threat to his powerful influence.

THE CITY OF HASTINGS

My initial visit to the City of Hastings was in the capacity of project manager and consultant to a real estate developer. I was very well received by the City's female Mayor, Lu Ann Stoffel and its council members. My position with the development firm was to identify cities who were in need of low to moderate income rental housing and the City of Hastings was very much in need with a vacancy rate of less than 2% in its City. It took only two visits in my position as project manager (for a male developer that I worked for) to get a resolution from City Council to develop a 96 unit housing complex. The City pledged to do all things necessary to facilitate the development with housing revenue bonds and agreed to establish a tax increment district to assist in funding, which would essentially reduce rental rates for the low to moderate income tenants. After the approval was received from the City, the male developer that I worked for decided against doing the project in the City of Hastings.

Since I was the project manager for this Edina, MN developer the Mayor of Hastings requested that I take on the project myself and I was promised the same full cooperation from the City for an identical project. I found Mayor Stoffel very persistence in promoting affordable housing in the City for her people. Not once did I hear her ask as to what kinds of people would occupy the housing like I did from the City's council. She had visited the project that I brokered as project manager for the Edina firm in the City of Champlin, MN. Mayor Stoffel was very much impressed with that project and wanted the same for Hastings. I took it upon myself to interview all council members personally to make sure that I had their full support as well and not just the mayor's word. All agreed to give me the same deal as given to the prior developer that I worked for previously.

What happened from the time that I made the initial presentation with the previous developer to the time I approached the City Council on my own behalf as a developer, is anyone's guess, but it was as if I was addressing an entirely new council. I expected a quick resolution as was the case previously, but instead it seemed that I had to first prove myself worthy of such a consideration.

Mayor Stoffel was not easily discouraged however, and together we sought out each councilmember to determine the cause of the stalemate. It became apparent that now council appeared to have a problem with a female developer. Of course, it wasn't my gender that caused them concern, according to council members, but rather it was a concern of their staff (David Osberg, City Manager and Shawn Moynihan, City Attorney). If there was a common theme by all those that the Mayor and I interviewed it was this, "I needed to bring a man on board". Never once, did we hear anything about a "qualified man", simply a "Man". So together the Mayor and I approached staff to determine their difficulty with dealing with a female developer and of course they denied any culpability and making such statements to council about refusing to deal with a female as a developer.

Other concerns expressed by members of council was that if tax-exempt bonds were used that would mean that 40% of the rental had to be pledged for low income people. Hastings's City Council saw that as bringing all the "Undesirables" to their 100% white community (with the exception of one black member) who worked for the Hastings School District. At this point in time, Hastings was a population of almost 25,000 people and only one minority in town, which was confirmed by the Mayor. In a taped council meeting one council member made the following statement, **"Ms. Fearing we are very much impressed with your proposed development but if we allow 40% of the rental pool for low-income that will bring in all the "'undesirables'", the Blacks, Hispanics, Indians, Welfare and God only knows what else".** Both the Mayor and I were horrified by those comments.

In another private meeting that I had with yet another councilmember, he voiced a similar reluctance in providing low income housing, but he targeted the "Hmong" population as the most undesirable. What ensued as the Mayor and I pursued this project was a two year dog-fight. It seemed that when we did have a meeting of the minds and I attempted to move the project forward we would encounter another stalemate. **When the Mayor and I attempted to review tapes of issues agreed upon, we would find that they had been either altered, erased or they simply disappeared.** The same was true for the Resolution that was drafted as an agreement between the City and me. **My copy of the Resolution had different language than what was agreed to and signed by members of Council. Of course, staff and Attorney Moynihan denied any wrongdoing even though they were responsible for drafting it**. The disparity in the Resolution contract was that the City was virtually not obligated to me at all. I could spend my money until hell froze over for various engineering, feasibility studies and whatever else the City deemed necessary. It was simply a means of extorting funds from me to pay for costs that should be borne by the City.

Every financial package that I proposed to the City was rejected and then they had the nerve to accuse me of not providing a workable financial package. Every package was workable, however, each financial proposal was premised on the City initiating a tax-increment district as they had agreed to do, but their fear of all the "undesirables" moving into their City prevented that district from being established. I did not have the statutory authority to initiate that process, only the City in its governing capacity.

Dealing with this racist and sexist City government became such an emotional drain; I became so exhausted and discouraged, I tried to cut my losses and simply walk away. Mayor Stoffel would not hear of that and was adamant that this project would move forward as her City was so desperately in need of housing. She had so much faith and confidence in me (a much welcomed gesture given the behavior of the reluctant staff) that I didn't want to disappoint her. My heart went out to her and I simply couldn't walk away, so I made a commitment to fight on. How this City treated me was described best by Mayor Stoffel in her testimony at the trial when she said this, "Marlena was tossed and thrown like a "'rag doll'" from one City official to another without any remorse for such uncivilized behavior".

Together the Mayor and I battled (a two year process—quite a contrast to the two week process for my male predecessor) until she lost the election and another Councilmember, Michael Werner was elected Mayor. He and I had become acquainted on more than one occasion. Mr. Werner made it known in a not so inconspicuous manner that he had a personal interest in me. Even with Mayor Stoffel's presence during our meetings, his eyes never left my chest. It was as if I had no face since he spoke directly to my breasts. Mayor Stoffel witnessed his conduct and she was apologetic for his behavior. I always dressed appropriately in a business suit, so his conduct was unwelcome and unbecoming, particularly for a representative of the City.

On another occasion, a more memorable one indeed, I was invited by Mayor Stoffel to meet an artist friend of hers (David Krech) at a popular restaurant in Hastings. As I was sitting and talking with the artist, councilmember, Michael Werner who subsequently became the new Mayor came over to my table and knelt down in front of me. He laid his head on my chest and groped at my thigh. I was shocked and speechless as well as all those who witnessed the event. Once I gained my composure I silently debated whether or not I should slap him. After a long thought, I decided against that notion.

Shortly after Mayor Werner took office, he called and asked me to meet him at Perkins Restaurant in Hastings, to talk about getting the project back on track. It was on Palm Sunday, no less. Mayor Werner, even as a council member had always been supportive of my project so I felt that I could overlook his crudeness and lack of manners and perhaps get a new fresh start. However, I was not prepared for what came out of his mouth. He wanted to make sure that he would get the credit for providing housing for the City and suggested that we essentially denounce and lay blame for the previous project's failure on former Mayor Lu Stoffel as well as what he referred to as her "handmaiden" the City's Planner (Edith Kaiser). I was offended and annoyed by that suggestion because both the Mayor and the City Planner had supported my project, but the best was yet to come. **He essentially promised me a project, but we would have to be "very discreet". We are talking about millions of dollars in federal funding and we are to be "very discreet"?**

I knew at that point that I would have to compromise my integrity to pursue this project. That was not "winning", but rather "losing". This was still a pig no matter how much lipstick you put on it. And how does one wrestle with a pig without getting dirty yourself? I don't know how long I sat and just stared at him in disbelief. What to do? The general contractor fee alone was $410,000., 1.8 million in tax credits (syndicated would result in $900,000. for construction costs) plus I would have retained 51% ownership of a 96 unit housing complex. In my mind, agreeing to that deal, I would be selling my soul to the devil. But the real loser in all of this was the people of Hastings as I felt they deserved better, but I didn't vote for him. I finally made it to my feet and walked away without looking back, knowing full well that I was walking away from a project that I had just wasted two years of my life trying to salvage something that was destined to fail because of racial intolerance and sexist attitudes. This is not a condemnation of the people of Hastings, but rather their elected officials.

My next visit with the tape of the "racial comments" was to the Minnesota Department of Human Rights. I had invited former Mayor Stoffel to come along as she witnessed the incident and heard the comments. We expected a full investigation into the City's denial of housing for minorities, but instead we got more excuses. Essentially, the investigator for Minnesota Department of Human Rights, (Barbara Forsland) found that the City of Hastings's comments were not racially motivated because the comments by the councilmember (even though in his position he decided who could or could not live in his lily-white community) had a right to "Freedom of Speech". How is it that the City is allowed "Freedom of Speech" for racial and gender discrimination, when my attempts at "Freedom of Speech" for writing a letter protesting eviction of blacks, got me 30 days in jail?

This has been a real eye opener as to how Cities can legally discriminate with impunity by manipulating and controlling who can or can not live in their community; a process sanctioned and acquiesced by those agencies established to discourage and prevent discrimination. Instead they get a "thumbs up". My sense is however, if this were a private firm instead of another government entity, action would have been taken against them. But I have found that there exists such camaraderie amongst government officials, whereby they protect one another, right or wrong. During this time frame, Arne Carlson was the governor (a Republican). I asked his office for an investigation into the matter. The resounding answer to me was that they had performed their investigatory process and found no wrong doing.

I eventually sued the City of Hastings for gender discrimination. All issues are well documented in **Dakota County District Court file # C3-96-1884.** It was evident that race of potential residents was a big factor in the refusal by the City to grant me the project; but I did not sue on issues of race. My attorneys were Leslie Linneman and Celeste Culburth. These ladies were excellent attorneys, but they weren't about to challenge a bigoted judge, particularly when he announced to them on the commencement of my trial, that he had awarded in their favor on another case they litigated before him. However, no order was written, the judge apparently withheld that to see whether or not my attorneys would appeal a "no" financial award in my case. This was in my opinion, a judicial "stick and carrot" approach that I found also used by other judges involved in the lawsuits brought against me.

Attorneys representing the City tried to discourage my attorneys from taking my case by attacking me, telling them that I was a felon and that I was going to be arrested for forgery. None of it true. But at least we had warning as to how they would structure their defense—by character assassination since they had no real evidence for their defense. On several occasions my attorneys found the City officials engaged in perjury, but when they attempted to make a court record of their perjured testimony, Judge Harvey Holtan refused to grant it. Instead he would ask my attorneys to present the question again. This went on sometimes with two and three attempts and with each attempt we heard a different version of the truth. The bias was obvious. Even though Judge Harvey Holton found a prima facie case (A finding of gender discrimination), I was awarded no damages since according to Judge Holtan, I had no previous experiences. **I had already been in the real estate business for 25 years as a real estate broker, developer, builder and consultant. I have always wondered what it would have taken to be sufficiently qualified in the eyes of this judge and if the requirements similar for a man?**

At trial, my experience was never even mentioned in court with the exception of the testimony of former Mayor Stoffel. She testified that she was very impressed with the project that I had negotiated and brokered in Champlin; and she wanted the same for the City of Hastings. **The City of Hastings had never offered my qualifications in any of its testimony as reason for denying the project. How could they, when I had the best consultants in the business representing me; Winthrop and Weinstein, legal consultants and Allison Williams, bonding consultants? The City's defense was always that I couldn't provide the financing.** When there was overwhelming proof that I had provided evidence that financing was available for me, the Judge had to agree with that. It was a victory of sort since the Judge did acknowledge gender discrimination when he found that there was **a prima facie case of gender discrimination**. But to expect a financial award from a Judge who refused to bite the hand that feeds him (the government) was perhaps a bit much to expect.

When my attorneys refused to file the appeal because they felt my case stood little chance with Judge Holtan's position at the appellate court, I filed and prepared my own brief. Interestingly, one of the judges assigned to hear my case at the appellate level was none other than Judge Harvey Holtan—as if he would consider overturning his findings at the district level. The lack of integrity by this judge speaks to his arrogance. I insisted that he recuse himself and he finally did but not before he successfully tainted the process with his influence, as the appeal was merely an exercise of futility for me. The final order was non-published and in reading the final result, it was obvious that if indeed it had been published the truth of the matter may just get unwanted attention.

THE CITY OF LAKE ST. CROIX BEACH

By the time that Hastings finished with me I had decided that if I wanted to continue in the development and construction business I had to change my tactical approach. Even though it was housing for low income people that I sought to build for, I realized that I simply could not withstand another financial beating in attempting another project that needed government involvement. I decided instead to purchase some acreage (15 acres) approximately 15 miles north of Hastings, in the City of Lake St. Croix Beach and build one-level luxury twin homes for sale to accommodate empty nesters and retirees with no age restrictions. At the time, I was still in my forties. I thought that this would be a nice project for me to build my nest egg and then retire early. So my anticipation was that I would live right at the model, and decorate it with all of my beautiful furnishings. Little did I know that the City of Lake St. Croix Beach would take control of my land, my project, my money, my freedom and my life. *The Mayor was a retired judge and evidence will show that he exercised his political and judicial connectedness as a political tool to punish me for my refusal to become a victim of his arrogance, hatred and abuse of power.*

When I made my initial presentation to the City with renderings depicting my proposed project to be known as the St. Croix "Villas", the comments were all favorable. In fact, the Planning Chairman, Rick Schletty requested of City Attorney, Mark Vierling, to advise me and my attorneys how to proceed with an application for formal approval to the City. Council woman, Barb Kopp who subsequently became a Mayor of the City, approached me after the meeting to express her desire to see such a project that I had proposed to be built in the City. In fact, she went on to say, "This is exactly the kind of project that the City wanted the prior land owners to build."

There was absolutely no indication of any negative feelings or any hostility directed towards me. Since I was received in such a positive manner by planning and council, I subsequently purchased the land as I thought from all appearances that I would be dealing with what seemed to be fair and reasonable people. It was a trap. Hindsight reveals that this City seized an opportunity for development of a much-needed community water shed to facilitate three surrounding cities at my expense. And they illegally took 1/3 of my property without any payment to me to facilitate that water shed.

What transpired in just a short period of time is suspect, and there is no doubt in my mind that acting Mayor John Jansen, City Attorney, Mark Vierling and City Clerk, Linda O'Donnell were very much involved in a scheme to intentionally and maliciously curtail my every effort to develop the 15 acres that I purchased in the City. All testimony and documented evidence prove that to be true.

From the time that the "Villas" project was proposed, there have been numerous elections. Faces changed, but the mean-spirited attitude toward me had only escalated. It is no secret to anyone familiar with Lake St. Croix Beach, that **Mayor John Jansen (former Washington county attorney and retired Minnesota State Administrative Judge)** essentially controls the town *then* and *now*. He hand picks his candidates mostly women, who will follow his directives. There is a method to his madness and that is to give the impression that he is open to treating women as "equals". Not true. He uses them to carry out his dirty deeds by empowering them so he can remain hidden.

There has been only one exception and that was one woman, who served as council woman and subsequently became Mayor (Dawn Beedle) until cancer forced her to retire. It is clear that council members and planning people alike defer their good common sense judgment to this man rather than question his integrity, motives or competence. Again, with the exception of Dawn Beedle who often expressed opinions contrary to his, but not without a fight for her right to do so. Like Mayor Stoffel in Hastings, Mayor Beedle always tried to do what was in the best interest of the City of Lake St. Croix Beach. She admitted on numerous occasions to my attorney and me (supported by an affidavit) that she has also felt discriminated against as a woman by this man, Mr. Jansen.

Excerpt from Affidavit of Mayor Dawn Beedle:

"I was required to sign a letter attacking and slandering Ms. Fearing which was drafted by City Attorney, Mark Vierling and mailed by the City of Lake St. Croix Beach to all members of the community."

"I feel I am in a very bad situation because I feel an obligation to protect the City's interest, but I refuse to break the law. I also feel that because of the conduct of these officials, our City and County government is losing tax revenue because of the denial of building permits. This must be remedied."

After the project was proposed and the land was purchased it became evident that the "Villas" was off to an ominous beginning and something was very much amiss. It was as if the City owned my land as they certainly controlled every aspect of it.

The closing transpired in September, 1992. I handed over my payment for the land in total and received a Warranty Deed. Later, I discovered that the City's Attorney, Mark Vierling contacted the Seller's attorney,(Mr. Simonet) and together in bad-faith they prepared a new Warranty deed, after the closing, solicited the prior owners (Johnson and Bjurlin) for their signatures, and changed the legal description without my knowledge. The legal description changed because the City took away a portion of land that I purchased. This is clearly fraud by definition, but the law doesn't apply to this City, since it is controlled by a mayor (John Jansen) who is an administrative judge for the State of Minnesota and a high ranking Republican with all the right connections.

It took almost a year for me to remedy this situation as the City decided to hold my title to the land hostage until I succumbed to all of their demands; which included giving up 1/3 of my land for a public watershed, a road and to pay delinquent assessments not paid by the previous owner. This slight error (deliberate or unintended) by the City Clerk is acknowledged in the Development Contract. Why should I be responsible for paying a $38,000. tax bill for taxes not owed by me? In the real estate business this is known as fraud and extortion, but for the City of Lake St.Croix Beach, it is business as usual. For over a year, I did not have the use of my money nor the land since it was tied up because of the City's corrupt endeavors.

For any prior male developer a one-time application fee of $500. was applicable. However, for me the initial application fee was $1,500. The fee was kept by the City for Attorney fees; however, the application itself was rejected supposedly because it was not properly completed, even though it was the City's attorney who instructed the completion of the form. A second application with a $1,500. fee according to the City's Attorney could not be submitted for six months. A new rule they wrote especially for me.

There were a lot of new rules written by this City that were not applicable to any previous all male developers. I had to provide a $90,000 Bond, $30,000 letter of Credit, $30,000. Cash Deposit, Proof of land ownership (difficult to do when they wouldn't allow me to record my deed) Upfront financial capacity to construct all 22 units without funding, forfeit 1/3 of my land for public use and then pay to construct a water shed to accommodate drainage for three neighboring Cities at an additional cost of $160,000, Pay a $15,000. Park dedication fee and provide demographic and density studies. In totality, they stole approximately $900,000. from me including land value and development costs.

Excerpt from Affidavit of Mayor Dawn Beedle:

"That as Mayor, I have reviewed the records and have discovered that Ms. Fearing was treated much differently than any prior developer."

In another letter to the City written by Attorney James Doran, he writes:

"There appears to be an absence of good faith on the part of the City and its officials. It seems that they are putting up more road blocks than the DOT (Department of Transportation) in July. In my opinion, Marlene is not receiving due process or equal protection. It leaves me to wonder if the City is being arbitrary and capricious in dealing with Marlene as a developer".

None of the above requirements were made of prior developers, all male, even though their developments were considered to be major developments while mine was so small it was considered a minor development. It was obvious that the City wanted to declare this project financially unfeasible before it even got off the ground. The numbers quoted may seem small, but these costs were for a project of almost fourteen years ago, when the proposed sales price of the twin homes were to be at $125,000 per unit.

The taking of my land for public use without just compensation is prohibited by a Supreme Court decision on June 24, 1994, whereby Chief Justice William Rehnquist, speaking for a 5-4 majority stated that, "forcing developers to give up their land violates the Fifth Amendment that private property (shall not) be taken for public use without just compensation". But the law doesn't seem to apply to the City of Lake St. Croix Beach which is depicted by all their deeds throughout this book. A subsequent federal judge (Joan Ericksen) appointed by George W. Bush in 2002, essentially rewrote this law in her recent finding when she refused to rule against the City when I sued to recoup my land value. So now we have a judge appointed by Bush (at a lower 8th circuit court) making findings which trump a ruling by the Supreme Court.

The next hurdle I faced was attempting to get a Development Agreement with the City, which took nearly two years. A typical time frame is two months for a project of this size, but again I had special rules written for me. All the above criteria were merely an appetizer for this City because they had their pallets wetted for a much larger bite of me. Records at the City reflect that no other project was ever encumbered by such outrageous financial demands and delaying tactics by the City as the "Villas" project. In fact, records also reflect that during this entire process two of my attorneys essentially walked away from negotiations due to the way I was being treated by the City.

In a letter to the City of Lake St. Croix Beach, dated January 20, 1994,

Attorney Robert Dickie writes, "Ms Fearing expects to be treated in a manner consistent with other developers in St. Croix Beach. It is becoming apparent to me a double standard has developed which results in considerable financial hardship. I have instructed Ms. Fearing that should the double-standard not disappear immediately, she should contact her litigation counsel and pursue judicial remedies."

In my mind litigation was not a viable option since Mayor Jansen had already threatened that if I had litigation on my mind, as I did in Hastings, I would never prevail as he personally knew every Judge in the County.

Excerpt from an affidavit of Theodor Perlinger: Dated March 18, 2002

"Because I was interested in what Ms. Fearing was proposing, I went to quite a few of the Council Meetings at Lake St. Croix Beach. I was appalled at the hostility directed at Ms. Fearing by the City particularly by City Attorney Mark Vierling and Mayor John Jansen"

"I recall one meeting that was quite memorable. Ms. Fearing's attorney, Bob Dickie was also present. The attitude and conduct at this meeting by the City was even more confrontational than in the past. It appeared to me that the City simply did not want to cooperate with Ms. Fearing."

"After the meeting, Mayor Jansen approached Ms. Fearing and stated, *'Let me warn you, Ms. Fearing, if you plan to sue like you did in Hastings, I know every Judge in this County'*. I was shocked that a Mayor would conduct himself in such a threatening manner."

Sometime in between the time frame of my initial presentation to the City of Lake St. Croix Beach and my attempts to acquire a Development Agreement with the City, it became apparent that there was somehow a joint effort between The City of Hastings and the City of Lake St. Croix Beach to mutually sabotage the "Villas" project.

While I had suspicions that there was this collusion between the two Cities, I had no evidence or proof as to who initiated those efforts until the summer of 1999, when I had discussions with two former Mayors of the City of Lake St. Croix Beach (Barb Kopp and Dawn Beedle) and both women informed me that the City of Hastings initiated contact with the City of Lake St. Croix Beach. It is my contention that the City of Hastings passed on their recipe for successful discrimination to the City of Lake St. Croix Beach. The projects were very different. The project proposed in Hastings was a rental and the proposed project in Lake St. Croix Beach was for sale. However, the discriminatory conduct by both cities is almost identical. Both Cities had a concern as to what kinds of people would occupy the housing.

Excerpt from Affidavit of Mayor Dawn Beedle (Dated September 14, 2000)

"I am aware that the City of Hastings was involved in Ms. Fearing's efforts to develop her land in Lake St. Croix Beach. Personal financial statements

and bank records of Ms. Fearing should never have been released without her expressed consent. Records will also indicate that no other developer was ever asked to submit any financial statements, much less any bank records indicating bank account numbers and balances".

It took three attorneys, to assist me in negotiating the development contract with the City of Lake St. Croix Beach for a minor sub-division consisting of approximately 15 acres.

The following excerpts taken from an affidavit prepared by Attorney James Doran, fairly sums up the negotiating process with this City:

"I attended many of the City Council Meetings with Ms. Fearing and I verily believe that there was never an attempt by the City to deal with Ms. Fearing in good faith. That is the opinion of two other attorneys that also were involved in attempting to negotiate with the City. The City attorney dictated the language to be inserted in the Development Agreement and the By-Laws. In fact, Ms. Fearing still has the original draft made by him as well as correspondence in which she protested the discriminatory language. The final documents were typed by another attorney working for Ms. Fearing, but the original draft form was written by the attorney for the City."

"All of Ms. Fearing's attorneys, including myself protested the language containing age restrictions, occupancy limitations and the no rental clauses because we felt this was targeting a certain class of people and therefore discriminatory. The response from both City Attorney and the Mayor was clear—without the language there would be no development contract. The fact that it took three attorneys to negotiate a minor sub-division such as the St. Croix Villas with the City is a statement in itself."

"While the City portrays Ms. Fearing as impossible to deal with, the truth of the matter is Ms. Fearing always relied on her consultants to do the negotiating, but the City knew that it was a female that gave direction. It was obvious by the demeanor and conduct of both the City Attorney and the Mayor that this was extremely bothersome for both of them. Both had difficulty in addressing Ms. Fearing with any civility or respect. The female Mayor also acknowledged to me on a couple of occasions that she also faced the same difficulty from these two individuals. She

even suggested in one such conversation that if Ms. Fearing had a male investor, that she should bring him to a council meeting so as to give her more credibility in the eyes of Mayor Jansen."

"While the City characterizes Ms. Fearing as contentious and incompetent, I feel the reverse is a better characterization from what I witnessed at not only the meetings, but subsequent conduct by the City and its representatives. For example, the City Engineer seemed to have difficulty determining his own specifications and the City attorney couldn't follow the resolutions and motions of the City council; and the mandates were constantly changing by these two key players for the City."

It became evident during the document production efforts in the lawsuit against the City of Hastings that somehow my personal financial records, including bank statements appeared in the Hasting's files without my authorization. At about the same timeframe a news article appeared in the Hastings Gazette about my proposed project in Lake St. Croix Beach. According to the article, Mayor Jansen offers comments about me personally that were not very flattering and he expressed concerns that my project would end up being rental housing. In my presentations to the City of Lake St. Croix Beach, there was never any representation or a suggestion of a rental project. **It became evident to me that the City of Hastings instilled the fear of "All those Undesirable People" moving into Lake St. Croix Beach. That was further confirmed by Mayor Kopp, wherein a taped conversation she admitted that my development agreement was drafted by the City attorney, Mark Vierling and Mayor Jansen, to prevent the "Hmong and the Blacks" from moving in.**

When I confronted Mayor Jansen about his comments to the Newspaper, he indicated to me that he had an obligation to keep out the riffraff from St. Paul. (Riffraff as described by Mayor Kopp to mean the "Hmong and Colored" or anything else) When I told Mayor Jansen that I had a Constitutional Right to develop my land, his response was that, "he too, had a Constitutional Right to believe that women do not belong in the construction business". (As a reminder, this guy was a former Washington County Attorney, a State Administrative Judge, a councilmember and Mayor). As the dialogue became more heated, he told me that, "as a former Washington County attorney, he knew every judge personally". I took that as a challenge to dare to seek judicial remedies for the way I was treated.

This was the second time that he made this threatening comment. I knew at that point that I was virtually powerless and had no choice but to succumb to this extortion and accept a contract with the City on their terms. But the sabotage of the "Villas" didn't end there. It was merely the beginning of a very long opera that many wished the fat lady would either sing or drop dead to end it all.

I received a Development Contract from the City on June 3, 1994, however, it became evident real soon that the City of Lake St. Croix Beach had no intention of honoring the Development Agreement and their harassment of me was only beginning. It seemed there wasn't anything that I could do right even if it was done at the direction of the City's own consultants. I believe much of this was for the benefit of discouraging other contractors from working with me. The construction of the public water shed was an absolute nightmare which can only be summed up by comments of the engineer that I hired to construct it. (Affidavit of LeRoy Nyhus)

After the City took my land for the water shed without compensation, they had the audacity to require that I pay for this monstrosity as a prerequisite to any building permits being issued to me. Their dilettantish conduct was no doubt a deliberate effort to block all attempts by me to perform on the development contract by issuing incorrect engineering reports, refusing construction permits for street and water lines. I was helpless to move forward without those permits as they would have sanctioned me with fines and penalties. As an example, the City engineer would issue incorrect elevations which required much more development costs due to the games that they played with my contractors. The City knew that the costs were astronomical for my contractors to come back repeatedly with their road graders, backhoes and other road building equipment. The games continued with the bituminous installation as well, i.e. the City engineer required that a curbing be placed across the driveways. After the residents complained to the City of their inability to enter their driveways, the City issued citations against me and I was required to remove all the bituminous curbing, even though it was installed as directed by the City's engineer.

Excerpt from a letter that I sent to the City Mayor dated October 23, 1995.

I am suffering delays in finishing Quasar Court. This is entirely due to unnecessary interference and erroneous information provided by your City Engineer. He determined that the level of the cul-de-sac was not high

enough and at his request I added five inches of grade material—at my expense. Now it has become obvious that his assessment was incorrect and I have to remove the same five inches of ground coverage before paving can be accomplished.

One would think that if indeed there was an error that by now it would be corrected. Not so. The next day I got news from my engineer that the City engineer made another error and of the five inches of ground that was removed, four inches must now be brought back prior to the bituminous application. Do I believe that this City engineer was that stupid and incompetent? No, this simply exemplifies the arrogance and deliberate attempts to steal my working capital and his refusal to deal with me with any civility. We finally got the correct elevation for the road but the sabotage doesn't end. The City engineer was adamant about a bituminous curbing being placed across all the driveways. My contractor insisted that would prohibit residents from entering the driveway, but the City's engineer refused to back down. When I inspected the installation I was absolutely livid and confronted my contractor. He responded to me by letter.

Excerpt from letter of Buck Blacktop, Inc.

I wanted you to know that the man representing the City told my foreman to pave with a continuous curb past the driveway and not to knock the curb down any lower at the driveways. In fact, he stated that is why they wanted the style of surmountable curb which we installed.

Excerpt from affidavit of Mayor Dawn Beedle:

"I also witnessed that City Engineers requested Ms. Fearing's bituminous people to apply a continuous bituminous curb across the driveways which subsequently prevented the residents from entering or exiting. Ms. Fearing, therefore, had to redo all of the driveways".

The following are some of the excerpts taken from the Affidavit of LeRoy Nyhus. Federal Court file # 04-CV-05127

"I was asked to attend City Council meetings with Ms. Fearing to get approval for her project. I found the City extremely hostile toward Ms. Fearing and a reluctance to even allow her on the council agenda. I recall at

one meeting that I attended, instead of being first on the agenda as "'new business'" we were placed at the end of the agenda. After approximately a two hour waiting period, Ms. Fearing was told by the Mayor (John Jansen) that she did not have her housing plans submitted. Ms. Fearing indicated that plans had been submitted to City Hall two weeks prior. Even though housing plans had nothing to do with the site plans, we were not allowed to address the council and had to reschedule. The City was aware that I lived approximately *two hundred miles* from Lake St. Croix Beach and I had made a long drive in vain."

"Ms Fearing had provided me with plat drawings from a previous developer (Johnson/Bjurlin) that made a proposal to the City under the name of Cedar Estates. Ms. Fearing used the same plat drawings because the City had already approved them. However, when Ms. Fearing took over the property, the requirements by the City changed. The size of the storm water holding pond increased significantly. The City engineer had stated that the low area on Ms. Fearing's property did not have an outlet until it overflowed Highway 95. *This is an erroneous statement*. The reason the City wanted to increase the holding size for the storm water was because the City allowed the area down stream from Ms. Fearing's property to be developed without proper drainage. Thus Ms. Fearing was required to furnish not only land for additional holding area for run off other than from her property, but was required to construct the holding pond at her cost without compensation from the City, just to pay for the City's previous ineptness. The first set of road plans were designed with a rural section. The City and their Engineer later demanded that the road be designed as an urban section."

"It was the City Engineer, that made these changes and recommendations to the City and refused to back off when I insisted that the ponding area requirement was grossly over-engineered. That Ms. Fearing's project contributed approximately 22% of the area to the drainage area and 78% came from property outside her development. The City's attitude was either comply with recommendations and specifications of their engineer or there was no project. I designed the developments plans according to what the City Engineer had dictated to me".

"This was one of the most difficult projects that I worked because it seemed that there was a deliberate effort to sabotage Ms. Fearing's efforts to timely complete Plan A of the project. I recall a comment made to me by the City Engineer, that 'I will not give that Ms. Fearing anything' and when he referred to Ms. Fearing it was not by her name but a very derogatory name for a female, and his actions proved that he meant every word because there was absolutely no effort to work or cooperate with Ms. Fearing, only to roadblock after roadblock. The impression that the City's engineer left me with was he did not want a female to succeed."

When the road was finally completed with the City engineer inspecting every aspect of construction, they refused to approve it and sign off. What this meant is that after dedicating another two acres of my land for a public street and spending approximately $160,000 to build this street, which I was to dedicate to the City, they thanked me by letting me know where I could "stick it". They refused to provide any street maintenance which meant that for two years I had to provide street maintenance for a public street. I felt obligated to do this because I did not want my buyers to suffer due to the City's ongoing wrath against me. This simply put, was another example of the vicious and mean-spirited conduct by this City to steal my working capital.

Excerpt from Affidavit of Attorney James

"I am convinced that there is nothing that Ms. Fearing could have done to please this City. This was déjà vu all over again as in the City of Hastings. The City of Lake St. Croix Beach seemed to follow the same play book that the City of Hastings drafted. Once again, Ms. Fearing was absolutely powerless in facing this well-connected political machine that had no regard for the law, property rights, or the rights of others. The conduct of many of these people was outrageous and unbelievable, particularly when you consider their positions of responsibility."

"It was obvious to me that the City of Lake St. Croix Beach had already determined in advance that they would not allow Ms. Fearing to succeed. That was also the opinion of others that were involved in this project. From what I observed, the City did everything in their power to sabotage, obstruct, impede her project and render her financially bankrupt which they certainly accomplished. The harder Ms. Fearing tried, the more determined the City became in their efforts to crush her. They accomplished their mission. For Ms. Fearing this was a Mission Impossible and I labeled it as such."

It is also my contention that the City of Lake St. Croix Beach did everything in its power to sabotage and financially bankrupt my development. Since they cannot impeach the evidence against them, all of which has been so well documented, their only recourse is to attempt to discredit me and paint me as incompetent. It is defense by character assassination rather than by contrary evidence. The pattern of attempting to make me the "The Villain" in order to exonerate themselves has been evident from the beginning.

Records reflect that they had absolutely no intention of dealing with me in good faith and placed as many roadblocks in my path as possible. I was virtually powerless in the face of such a formidable force. It was their conduct that forced my project into bankruptcy. The conduct of this City and that of their planners has literally obliterated this project and destroyed the home values due to the City's negative propaganda associated with my development.

The following is how the City of Lake St. Croix Beach deprived me of my basic Constitutional Rights.

1. Even though I had a contract to develop my land, the contract was illegal because it was a mandate to deny housing for certain groups of people. HUD, Fanny Mae and the U.S. Justice Department (Under Clinton Administration) indicated that the contract as drafted by the City was not enforceable because the intent was to discriminate and therefore illegal. It did not meet any of the HOP or HOPA (special provisions provided for "senior only" housing) exclusions as defined by federal housing law to make it a senior complex. The City Attorney, Mark Vierling and Mayor John Jansen were adamant upon inserting age restrictions, limitation on occupancy and a "no rental" clause even though as attorneys, they knew full well this was discriminatory and therefore, illegal.

     Because the language was discriminatory, I could not get financing for my buyers because it violated banking laws as well. After a year long battle, I was finally able to get a banker in Stillwater, MN to submit my development to get HUD underwriting. Attorneys for HUD and Fanny Mae made a determination that since the contract with the City was illegal on the face of it, the contract was not enforceable, so they granted me approval for funding on the entire project. (Reminder, this contract was written by the City's attorney, Mark Vierling and Mayor John Jansen, an attorney for 50 plus years.) A reasonable mind could only conclude that this was yet another attempt to derail my ability to market my townhomes.

In a taped conversation with former Mayor Barb Kopp, she acknowledged the language was inserted by Attorney Mark Vierling and Mayor John Jansen because the intent was to "Keep out the Hmong and Colored."

2. The City essentially attempted to force me to violate federal housing laws by the way they conducted themselves in refusing to issue building permits when my buyer was black. When I would confront the City about the permit denial they always had an excuse; I owed them money, I didn't pay my taxes, etc. etc. None of it true. If it were true, it would mean that all of the permits that were issued to the white buyers should have been denied issuance for the same reasoning. When I attempted to change the by laws as President of the Association, the City refused to allow it since they also had control of the Association because they made the association by laws a part of the development contract. Clearly, much thought went into drafting the development contract as they put controls on everything from who could live at the project to whom I could sell to if I should want to sell the project. They (City attorney and Mayor Jansen) made sure I could not get away until they had confiscated all of my assets.

3. I needed permits from the City to install water lines, construct the road and build the water shed. They delayed issuing those permits until the time allowed for construction per the developer agreement had expired, so then they could attempt to pull my $90,000 performance bond. Then they sued me for the money. Fortunately, the bond company had an aggressive attorney and they did not succeed. We eventually ended up with a mediation agreement, but still the City refused to even comply with that (a court ordered agreement). Once again, the City considers themself to be above the law.

4. When I discovered for the second time that a building permit was denied for a black person I again confronted the City and filed a report (as I am required to do as a housing developer and according to fair housing laws) with the Minnesota Department of Human Rights (MDHR) and the Federal Housing and Urban Development (HRA). Federal Housing law requires that I report discrimination, yet when I did I was retaliated and attacked by the City and its agents for reporting. Apparently the fair housing laws pertain to all citizens but excluding government officials from any obligation or enforcement of those laws.

MINNESOTA DEPARTMENT OF HUMAN RIGHTS (MDHR) FEDERAL HOUSING AND URBAN DEVELOPMENT (HUD)

It took both the MDHR and HUD approximately two years to investigate because of the paper trail created by the City to smoke screen their illegal conduct in this matter. Creating confusion was all part of the tactic to facilitate their discriminatory efforts, both gender and racial. The head investigator for the State of Minnesota was a veteran investigator of 26 years. She found "Probable Cause" for both racial and gender discrimination. She indicated to me that in her 26 years of investigations, she had never encountered a case this egregious in its discriminatory tactics. The investigator for HUD was also appalled by the conduct of this City and he indicated that he would recommend to the U.S. Justice Department that they proceed with legal prosecution of the City for their discrimination. **The U.S. Justice immediately froze the City's funds and I was told that prosecution of the City was in the works. This was under the Clinton Administration.**

MDHR

The finding by the MDHR was that both gender and racial discrimination had occurred and a Probable Cause Finding was issued. The Memorandum Stated as follows:

In paragraph one of the Memorandum, the MDHR writes of the conflicts between the charging party (Marlene) and the respondent (The City) over a number of issues and events relating to her business as a real estate developer. These difficulties have included special assessments, zoning and planning changes, public improvements and maintenance of them, construction delays, engineering changes, and denial of building permits. The charging party (Marlene Fearing) asserts that most of these difficulties have been unnecessary or were made particularly onerous for her, because of her gender and/or in reprisal for her having complained that the respondent and its agents have discriminated against her and against two prospective buyers who are African-American, for whom she was unable to build units. The investigator writes,

FINDING: "There appear to be no substantial disputes as to the course of events giving rise to this charge; rather, the issue in contention is the reasons for them. Investigation of these charges focused primarily on events in 1999 and since then. One older example of the respondent's (City) differential treatment of the charging party serves to illustrate that the discriminatory treatment dates back several years, however, and shows that this treatment has continued up to and including events alleged in these charges."

In paragraph two of the Memorandum, the MDHR writes: "A determination that there is probable cause to believe discrimination occurred can be made when the evidence shows '"Treatment so at variance with what would reasonably be anticipated absent discrimination that discrimination is the probable cause explanation. To find that an unfair discriminatory practice has occurred, the record must establish either 1.) An adverse difference in treatment of one or more persons when compared to the treatment accorded others similarly situated except for the existence of an impermissible factor such as sex, or 2.) Treatment so at variance with what could reasonably be anticipated absent discrimination that discrimination is the probable explanation.'" City of Minneapolis v. Richardson, 239N.W. 2d 197,202 (Minn. 1976)."

FINDING: *The treatment accorded the charging party (Marlene Fearing) in this situation clearly meets the court's standard as "treatment so at variance . . . . that Discrimination is the probable explanation."*

In paragraph three of the Memorandum with regard to denial of building permits for blacks, the MDHR investigator writes, "The respondent (City) maintains that it had no knowledge of the race of the prospective buyers in April and August of 1999."

FINDING: Investigation results were persuasive of the charging party's contention that this was known, and that it was a factor motivating the denial of the building permit application. *The respondent's different responses on these requests is so at variance with what would reasonably be anticipated absent discrimination, that discrimination is the probable explanation.*

In paragraph four of the Memorandum, the MDHR investigator writes this: The respondent and charging party had disagreed as to the amount she owed the City for administrative, engineering and legal expenses, as provided in their development agreement. That agreement also had a provision that any such disputes would be resolved through arbitration, and they had agreed to submit this matter to an arbitrator. In September of 1995, the City Council passed a motion directing the City attorney to initiate arbitration to establish the amount due. The City attorney, however, failed to follow this directive, and no arbitration was commenced to resolve the dispute. The development agreement also required the charging party to post a performance bond that would cover any expenses the respondent incurred if the charging party failed to meet her financial obligations to the City. Although the respondent contended throughout the period in question that the charging party owes it several thousand dollars for various expenses, it has never attempted to collect by invoking the performance bond, nor did it file a claim as a creditor in the charging party's bankruptcy proceedings.

FINDING: *"The respondent's (City) failure to proceed with arbitration, despite its agreement to do so and its directive to the City attorney, and its failure to attempt to secure the monies it claims are owed by invoking the performance bond, are so at variance with what would reasonably be anticipated absent discrimination, that discrimination is the probable explanation."*

The Minnesota Attorney General's Office contacted me and requested a meeting to see if a settlement could be reached prior to initiating prosecution. That idea was short lived as the City brought in their high-priced, judicially and politically connected attorneys to protest the findings. According to the Attorney General's Office, they could not prosecute without the authority of the MDHR, because it is a politically appointed position. Even though there was no additional evidence entered in, the MDHR reversed the Probable Cause Findings. I was told by the head investigator that if the findings were reversed, it would be because of political maneuvering and not because of lack of evidence to substantiate that discrimination did take place. So essentially this became a political issue rather than an issue of civil rights violations and civil rights laws were not enforced. In fact a year later when Michael Aymar took over the project, the MDHR told him (as reported in findings by the MDHR) that the contract with the City was discriminatory and he had to abandon the age and occupancy restrictions. This further exemplifies the blatant disregard by the MDHR for my constitutional rights by playing politics with my civil liberties and refusing to enforce housing laws when it is a government entity that is the perpetrator. Bottom line, the MDHR acknowledges discrimination and then changes their finding due to politics. Later, they once again declare the contract with the City discriminatory and insisted that Michael Aymar could not enforce the restrictions as outlined in the development contract. *Not to worry on this minor detail since the City has another plan—bring in the judiciary to aid in their discrimination by changing and destroying the evidence and proclaiming the project "A senior housing project". Never mind that the change would violate State and Federal housing laws by making it senior housing—the end justifies the means—keeping the City "All white". Only the blacks were evicted and all whites under 55 received "special waivers" to remain. That's justice in Lake St. Croix Beach, Mn., County of Washington.*

HUD

HUD also found probable cause on both racial and gender discrimination and forwarded the file to the U.S. Department of Justice for prosecution.

In 2000, under the Clinton Administration, the U.S. Justice Department also determined that there was 'probable cause' for both gender and racial discrimination against the City of Lake St. Croix Beach. I was told that they were placing a very high priority on this case since it was a government entity that was the perpetrator. The prosecuting attorney worked very hard and diligently to prosecute this case. The City's bank accounts were immediately frozen. I recall very late calls into the evening from the prosecuting attorney when she had questions on the file and needed clarification. Unfortunately it became a political issue as well at the U.S. Department of Justice when Bush came into power. The case was closed very quietly with no explanation. How did it become a closed case under the Bush Administration from a case urgent in need of prosecution under the Clinton Administration is the big question?

According to retired City Mayor Dawn Beedle, John Jansen (man who has controlled the town for 6 decades) was absolutely **"consumed with rage"** and vowed to **"get me"** for complaining to the U.S. Justice Department. She forewarned me that I should always keep my doors and windows bolted because she felt Mr. Jansen had the capacity and power to retaliate against me by planting drugs or having me injured. Interestingly, a local attorney also forewarned me with a similar concern for my safety. That seemed to be the next power play, to "get me".

RETALIATION BY THE ESTABLISHMENT

Once U.S. Justice closed the file, the City perceived that as a signal that they could violate State and Federal laws with impunity—and that gave them the green light to assault and retaliate against me even further.

Clearly, directives were given by the City to two of their planners, their attorney and others to initiate a terror campaign against me in an attempt to force me out from my project and out of business. I was viciously attacked and vilified by this City and their hooligans. They included City Planners Mary Parr and Robert Swenson, their attorney Jon Erik Kingstad, newly appointed Developer Michael Aymar and others. They all knew what their assignments were and they wasted no time in initiating the process as described by witnesses in their affidavits later in this documentary.

Using retaliatory measures against me for reporting discrimination is a federal offense. But once again, this City is above the law.

Under Federal law Title 18 U.S.C. Section 241 (Conspiracy against Rights) and Section 242 (Deprivation of Rights). "Under Color of Law", this statute makes it a crime for any person acting under color of law, statue, ordinance regulation, or custom to willfully deprive or cause to be deprived from any person those rights, privileges, or immunities secured or protected by the Constitution and laws of the U.S.

(Again, as a reminder) Mr. Jansen, the City's Mayor is a Minnesota State Judge who was the main principle architect in the campaign to destroy me and he did it under the auspices of "Color of Law". The same is true for the Washington County District Judges and the Federal Judges

who refused to allow me a jury trial and denied me due process under Constitutional Law.

The following was a result of the U.S. Justice Department's failure to uphold the law and prosecute for civil rights abuses by City, County and State Government.

1. The City sold my property without my approval to a developer, Michael Aymar, who has a long history of acquiring property fraudulently, stripping the equity and filing for bankruptcy.
2. The City initiated a "Terror Campaign" against me by destruction of my properties and physical assaults and attacks on me and my family by City Planners to instill terror and force me to move. The City, the County and State alike, refused to give me any protection under the law. When I attempted to get a protection order on three separate occasions from the local Washington County courts, I was denied such protection. On my third attempt, I was told if I made any more attempts for a protection order, I would get an order for contempt.
3. The City took control of my property with bogus and fraudulent lawsuits initiated by City Planners—living at the development (Mary Parr and Robert and Arlene Swenson and their attorney Jon Erik Kingstad) Lawsuits were designed and initiated against me and my corporation to encumber my properties, aided by corrupt judges in the City's pocket. Door after door was closed to me at the judicial process, first at district court, appellate court and then the federal courts. That was the biggest disappointment of all, when it came to rights guaranteed to me under the Constitution, none existed. The conduct of the judges was akin to that of criminals; i.e., suborning perjury, changing evidence, ignoring the evidence, destroying evidence, legislating from the bench and ignoring the "Rule of Law", under the "Color of Law" and denying me access to the court.

The scam was to make it appear complicated and confusing so the paper trail could not lead back to the City or the judges complicit in this corrupt process. The attacks on me were occurring simultaneously; destruction of my property, lawsuits, theft of my property and attacks on me personally. Attorney James Doran described it best when he said,

"This was a well-planned and executed modern day high-tech lynching by government officials".

MICHAEL AYMAR

After I filed a complaint with the Minnesota Department of Human Rights and HUD, the City of Lake St. Croix Beach again retaliated against me and refused to issue building permits; at the same time refusing to allow me to sell my project to other developers. I tried to sell my property and simply walk away from this insanity, but the City prevented me from accomplishing that as well. Every purchase agreement I wrote the City would sabotage the sale. That was until Michael Aymar came into the picture. Who recruited who, I am not sure. But in any event when I signed a purchase agreement I didn't know I was dealing with Mr. Aymar because the offer was brought to me by another accomplice of Aymar's, Gifford Vincent. I only found out about the connection between the City and Mr. Aymar during a conference call with the U.S. Attorney in D.C. (prosecuting this case against the City) and attorney James Doran when we were informed that the City had a buyer for my land.

When I did a research on Mr. Aymar's background, I discovered that he was well known for his land thievery. He buys property on a land contract, strips the equity by placing fraudulent mortgages with the help of a title company, First Advantage Title (President, Thomas Whiteis) and then files for bankruptcy. When I discovered that Aymar was just another City appointed stooge (amongst many) who made a deal with the City to take my property, I tried to cancel the contract. Aymar sued me for specific performance and I had no choice but to proceed with the sale. A year later he sued me to get out of a contract that he sued me to get.

Some would say, how can a City sell property when it doesn't belong to them? The City's interpretation of the development contract, written by the City, is that it prevents me from selling to a buyer of my choice. Technically, that is not correct, but I found it fruitless to challenge this City's interpretations.

The contract states that a new developer would have to agree to the same terms as I did; not that the City would have to approve the buyer. The City, however, insisted that they had the right to choose the buyer and they sabotaged every sale that I had negotiated. There indeed was a reason for their madness. The motive by this City was clear—to retaliate and punish me for challenging them on their sexist and racist practices. They obviously could have cared less about the success of the project as their main focus was to destroy me and anything else that got destroyed in the process was only collateral damage to them. The fact that the entire City, County and State suffered due to tax revenues lost by the devaluation of home values which has resulted in a lower tax base was not a consideration. Minimally $50,000. plus per year could have been generated from real estate taxes from the Villas project. The 'big loser' in all of this, however, was the people of Lake St. Croix Beach because the short fall was taxed to the rest of homeowner's. Washington County School District also suffered revenue losses as well. The conduct of this City and that of their planners has literally obliterated this project and destroyed the home values due to the City's negative propaganda associated with my development. Where are the Washington County Commissioners to oversee such an assault on the tax revenue base and waste of taxpayer dollars? Apparently too busy worrying about their next re-election to be bothered with such nonsense, so they cozy up and present a unified front of no wrong doing.

It took me two years to get building permits from the City. In contrast, Mr. Aymar received building permits in less than a month. He wasted no time with construction. The first unit constructed was supposed to be my new townhouse which had been negotiated as part of the agreement in the sale of my property. The contract between Mr. Aymar and I stated that there were to be no mortgages taken against my properties until all payments to me were complete.

I discovered a short time later that Mr. Aymar along with another accomplice of his Mr. Tom Whiteis, President of the 1st Advantage Title Company facilitated efforts to not only mortgage my properties, but took title illegally to my property using third party shell corporations known as Transaction Real Estate, LSCB,LLC, Minnesota Real Estate Specialists, Pro-Action Mortgage, and Property Holdings, LLC and others. Since Mr. Whiteis was the closer of the original sale of the properties between Mr. Aymar and myself, it was Mr. Whiteis's responsibility to record the documents.

A real estate closer is supposed to be unbiased and neutral to both parties. In this instance it is clear that Mr. Whiteis was in Aymar's pocket. He was the main architect in drafting the various documents along with Aymar's attorney, John Westrick illegally transferring titles to third parties when I was the still the owner. The very fact Mr. Whiteis was paid some $15,000 as a closing fee when most closing fees are typically $350. to $500. on such a transaction, speaks volumes. Clearly, he was complicit in aiding Mr. Aymar with taking mortgages illegally against my property because my interest in the contract was not recorded at the county. Therefore, the mortgage bankers that placed the original mortgages or purchased them on the secondary market had no knowledge of my interest in some of these properties. While Mr. Whiteis was writing title policies on the properties involved, he was committing fraud when he knew full well of my interest in the property and did not disclose that to the bank's underwriters. I reported this to the Minnesota State Licensing and they did nothing to correct this thievery by Mr. Aymar and Mr. Whiteis. They both hold Minnesota licenses to steal property with the acquiescence of the Minnesota State Licensing Division.

When I reported this to the Washington County Sheriff's Department, I was told that this is a civil matter and they could do nothing to help me. What I found even more interesting is that there was no report filed at the Sheriff's office of my complaint about theft of my property by Mr. Aymar and his accomplices through equity stripping. Mr. Aymar's team consisted of lst Advantange Title Company run by Tom Whiteis, Mr. Aymars two brothers Marc Aymar and David Aymar, Minnesota Real Estate Specialist and Pro-Action Mortgage, Brian Williams of Great Northern Financial Group, Contractor Tony Polaia of Vista Construction, Attorney John Westrick, Gifford Vincent, Marco ironi, Sean Maynard, Aaron Schwinn and Gerald Sadoff, CPA.

The City's chosen developer (Mike Aymar) subsequently abandoned the project after completing 8 units, but not before mortgaging property that I still owned; leaving me with the task of fighting over ownership with the banks. To make matters even worse, he filed for bankruptcy in September, 2003, to defraud me on a $600,000. Judgment that I was awarded against him in March, 2003, when he neglected to show up in court.

Never, mind that little "slip up" because Judge Doyscher will see to it that I don't collect on the judgment in any event. Not only does Judge Doyscher allow Mr. Aymar and his goons to commit fraud and perjury in his courtroom repeatedly; but then he subsequently gives my property to Mr. Aymar when evidence and testimony was clear that my property was taken by fraudulent means. There was no level playing field in his courtoom. Given the fact that this judge also has a background in real estate makes his conduct even more egregious. I had the law and the evidence on my side and still could not get a fair ruling from this judge.

RETRIBUTION FOR REFUSING
TO EVICT BLACKS

Shortly after turning the project over to Michael Aymar, I left my townhouse in Minnesota and moved to Arizona for the winter. I had given full power of attorney to GNA (Investigation and collection firm) to do all things necessary in my behalf. By this point in time, my health had deteriorated significantly from all the stress in having to deal with all of this madness. For three months, my days were spent in a state of catharsis just staring into the Catalina Mountains from the back porch of my townhouse in Arizona; meditating, praying, reading and trying to put myself together emotionally, psychologically, physically and spiritually. It was extremely difficult for me to comprehend and absorb all that had already happened to me, not knowing that the worst was yet to come.

When I returned for the holidays, my neighbors had informed me that City Planners, Mary Parr and Robert Swenson, were holding private meetings guised as association meetings and scheming to have the black family evicted. As the President for the Association, I met with the board and we voted to have Mary Parr removed from the Board for her illegal racist activities. Therefore, she no longer had any authority to represent the Association in any capacity. Robert and Arlene Swenson had already been evicted from the Association for non-payment of assessments. However, on their own and without Association authority, they solicited with help from the City and their attorney, Jon Erik Kingstad to devise and arrange a plan to sue me on behalf of the Association and have the black people removed. The Association by-laws strictly prohibited any litigation unless approved by all voting members.

Two things happened in the summer of 2003, that the City could no longer tolerate; not only was Fearing back in town, but Blacks were moving in, and

Fearing was blocking efforts to have them evicted. That seemed to be the deciding factor in declaring war on me. At about the same time frame several other residents called a meeting and asked me to attend. Several homeowner's had informed me that according to Mary Parr something "Really Big" was coming down and the City was giving her and Bob Swenson full support to get rid of me. According to the residents of the villas, the plan being schemed by City Planners Parr, Swenson and their attorney Kingstad included gaining control of the remainder of my land, my house, and my cars. They had already decided amongst themselves who would get my real estate and my other assets.

They went on to say that Parr and Swenson hired an attorney, Jon Erik Kingstad (who was getting assistance from the City's attorneys) to help them. And efforts were being made to solicit others at the Villas to join them in suing me. In attendance at this gathering was Kay Smith, Edith Ryan, Diana Winters, Theodor Perlinger and myself. At this meeting, these people also asked me to stay and take back the project and have it completed. I indicated that unless they gave affidavits to document what was taking place, a written letter to the City protesting the City's conduct, as well as their support in fighting yet another attack from this City, I would not be interested in finishing the project. They agreed and attached are the affidavits and letter in support of what was transpiring in an all out effort by Parr, Swenson and the City to retaliate against me. Excerpts from the affidavits indicate that if there's a common theme, it's to "Get Me" by taking all of my assets. I'm described as a "nobody" and a "nothing" and they are going to take away all of my property and get me out of town. My sin was that because I had gotten the MDHR and HUD involved, Blacks are now moving in. For that I am to blame, according to the allegations.

In an excerpt from a letter written by a Villas resident, Kathryn Smith to Lawyers Professional Responsibility Board she writes as follows:

"On July 22, 2003 and during the annual meeting of the Association, I was voted to be the Secretary Treasurer. While serving in this capacity, during several working sessions with Mary Parr and Arlene Swenson, I had asked repeatedly what this lawsuit was all about. I received the answer that they could not talk about it, as it had nothing to do with the Association and that it was THEIR lawsuit and thus should not involve me at all. They did however, mention quite explicitly how they were going to split up Marlene Fearing's assets after their win—i.e. who would take

which car and who would take her properties in Arizona and Mexico. I am willing to submit an affidavit to this effect."

"I stressed to Mr. Kingstad that I did not want to become a part of this litigation and in fact wrote a letter to him to this extent. It is obvious to me, that Mr. Kingstad had a conflict of interest by representing both Parr/Swenson and the Association by suing other Association members. I have since looked at the Association Bylaws many times and nowhere could I find a clause that legal action can be brought by the Board in a case as this, without specific approval of the Association members."

ASSAULTS, TERROR AND DESTRUCTION

My return back to Minnesota can only be described as "Hell on Earth". My market signs had already been cut down by Mary Parr with the help of her two grandsons on the previous Thanksgiving Day. While most Grandmothers are preparing a Thanksgiving Day feast for their families, Mary Parr was teaching her grandsons how to commit a felony. These signs due to the art work involved were valued at $8,500. They had survived numerous attacks previously of defacing and removal of my phone numbers, which I had repeatedly repaired. So this time, she had to make it final with her chainsaw and cut them into pieces. She proudly displayed them in her garage for days with the garage door open to show the world of her great accomplishment.

Sheriff Deputy Becky Engel did the investigation and she reported that Mary Parr told her that the City of Lake St. Croix Beach told her to destroy my signs. When Sheriff Deputy Engel wanted to file charges against the City, the story then changed. Mary Parr then indicated that it was the Homeowner's Association that gave her permission to do it. I was still the president of the Homeowner's Association and there was no such resolution to remove or destroy the signs. In any event neither the City nor the Homeowner's Association had the authority to destroy my signs but more importantly nobody was charged with the crime of destruction of my property which is a felony based on the cost to replace them.

This was only the beginning of what was in store for me from these deranged and hateful people. My windows were knocked out, some costing $9,000. each to replace, water fountains broken, bird baths smashed, they destroyed my vacant lots with a backhoe under the auspices of grounds keeping. They removed not only all the wild flowers that were planted but they also removed all the top soil and left ridges in some places over a foot deep. Again this was reported to the Sheriff's Department. Instead of the City and its planners being charged with criminal trespassing and destruction, I was threatened with incarceration if I attempted to prevent their lawn maintenances. This outrage was so unbelievable that even some of the residents decided to write a letter and protest their conduct. I have enclosed photos of vacant land before and after their vandalism which they declared as "lawn maintenance".

This is an excerpt of a letter written to the City by some residents who were outraged by the attacks on my project by the City's planners. Written to City of Lake St. Croix Beach—notarized signatures by Theodor Perlinger, Edith Ryan, Diana Winter and Kathryn Smith (All residents of St. Croix Villas)

"Dear Mayor and Members of Council:

The undersigned wish to voice our grievances and protest the ongoing harassment directed at this project and its original developer, Marlena Fearing. It has become obvious, the City, its agents, Mary Parr and Bob and Arlene Swenson are carrying out vindictive activities directed at her in an all out effort to "Get her". The latest being the mowing of the wildflowers including the State flower, on lots 1, 2 and 3. How can the City find these flowers objectionable when it's the same seeding that Ms. Fearing was required to plant, at the direction of the City, which is also growing in now the City owned holding pond?

While the City continues to hold itself above the law, your obvious contempt of Marlena Fearing and efforts to retaliate against her is spilling over and infringing on our rights and freedoms of home ownership. The City's continued efforts to destroy this project has also destroyed our values and ability to market our properties when there is such negative stigma attached to this development. We want the City to clean up this eyesore created by the cutting of the wildflowers at the City's expense. Most of us have witnessed for years, your mean-spirited conduct directed at Ms. Fearing and we have said and done nothing, but you have surpassed any reasonable doubt as to where the problems lie at this point. It bogs the minds of reasonable people as to why this City insists on destroying such a wonderful development when it's such an asset to this community?"

After city's lawn maintenance
This is not cutting, but a callous disregard for my property.
There is no excuse for this kind of destruction.

This is what vacant lots looked like prior to City's Maintenance. The flowers consisted of beautiful lavender, pink, yellow, white and blue wildflowers.

When my grandson's life was threatened and placed in danger by a hateful act committed by a representative of the City, Robert Swenson, I swore I would someday expose these spineless cowards. To attack a nine year old boy simply because of his ethnicity is indicative of the hatred and ignorance that exists there. This is the same individual that also told my grandson that if he didn't get back to his Grandma's house, that he would call the klu-klux-klan on him. My grandson was only 6 years old at the time. This, I think quite aptly portrays the racial hatred by these people. How can this be happening in America was the question asked repeatedly by a majority of the St. Croix Villa residents?

As my health took a steady decline I realized that I needed more help than just legal. I hired several investigators to try to get to the source of the problem and attempt to collect money that was owed to me. I hired GNA(Gauthier, Nechodom and Anderson). I felt it a good choice since Mr. Gauthier was a former U.S. Marshall and knew the workings of the court system. Mr. Gauthier acknowledged on numerous occasions how appalled he was of the corrupt events that were taking place. He had made numerous attempts to levy on assets owned by Mr. Aymar only to find that my own attorney, Mr. Chad Lemmons had not recorded the judgment that I had against Mr. Aymar. It seemed as though my own attorneys were doing more to harm me than to defend or protect me, excluding attorney James Doran. James Doran has been a long-time friend of mine (33 years) and represented me in both business and personal issues. Unfortunately he could not represent me in some of these cases since he had to serve as a witness to many of the events.

The events that followed are forever imbedded in my mind and still haunt me today. This was a well organized attempt to instill such fear into me that I would just pack and leave the community. Planners for the City, Mary Parr and Robert Swenson lived half way up the street from me, while I lived at the end of the cul-de-sac. There was no need for them to come to the end of the cul-de-sac, but they worked out a routine between themselves to stalk and harass me on a daily basis. Parr or Swenson would twice daily, in the morning and again toward evening circle the front of my townhouse. Sometimes they would take photos of me or just sit in their car and other times they stood at the end of my driveway just staring at me. Sometimes they even gestured to me with their middle finger as they displayed their IQ. I called the sheriff on numerous occasions and sometimes they came out to file a report, but mostly they ignored me. Only once did an officer file a report against both Parr and Swenson for trespassing, but mostly my complaints were ignored. I was told that they could do nothing to stop their stalking since it was a public street. I insisted that public street or no public street I was being stalked and harassed. That seemed to make no difference. I still received no protection.

Then it escalated to peeking into my windows at night and objects being thrown at my home to awaken and frighten me. I always called the sheriff's department and sometimes they came, but mostly they did nothing. I truly believe that the Washington County Sheriff's deputies wanted to help me, but they were as frustrated as I was because they knew that their efforts to enforce the law were a waste of time. Washington County has many good and honest law enforcement officers, but they are not given the support they need when it is government officials violating the law. Many deputies told me that neither the City nor the County would prosecute these people since they were agents of the City and therefore a conflict.

I recall one evening when my Grandson and a friend (Chris) stayed over and they were awakened by someone standing outside their window peaking in at them with a flashlight. Again I called the Sheriff's department and this time they did come out but I don't know if they filed a report or not, but in any event I heard nothing more about the incident.

Then the phone began ringing with just heavy breathing and other times *I was called a "Nigger Lover" and a "White Nigger", despicable words of hate simply because I defended and refused to discriminate against minorities as a housing developer. (*Such messages were even placed in my mailbox) I decided to start taping the calls. One day I received a threat from a disguised muffled voice that threatened "I know where you live 'Bitch' and I am going to get you". I immediately called the sheriff's department and I played the tape for the deputy. He told me that he couldn't do anything about it and that I would have to call the phone company to report it.

I knew that this was coming from Robert Swenson as threats from him were already evidenced, even in the presence of his attorney Jon Erik Kingstad and my attorney Mark Kallenbach at the Washington County Court house. After one hearing, Mr. Swenson informed my attorney Mr. Kallenbach, which according to Mr. Kallenbach, Mr. Swenson repeated three times, that "Fearing will be seeing Jesus soon if she doesn't stop calling the Sheriff's Department". Kallenbach informed me of the incident, but did nothing to report it to the courts or Sheriff's officials.

Parr and Swenson had become so emboldened and their attacks on me only escalated since they already knew that they could break the law with impunity as operatives of the City they were protected from prosecution as well as the City. There were numerous attacks on me which were reported as the following will indicate.

One day as I had driven into the entry of the development I had noticed that a contractor, hired by Mary Parr and Robert Swenson was once again trespassing on my property to do their scheduled lawn maintenance. Typically a cutting mower is used for lawn maintenance, but this guy was using a backhoe to destroy the top soil. I ordered him off of my land. Apparently Swenson had observed what I had done and he got into his car and came directly toward me (in my lane) so fast that smoke and screeching sounds were coming from his tires. At the last second, he swerved and avoided hitting me head on. Two of the residents were walking and observed it all. They called the sheriff and reported what they observed, that Mr. Swenson was in such a fit of rage that they were sure he would have run me over if not for their presence. Was Mr. Swenson prosecuted for his attempt to take my life using his vehicle as a deadly weapon? Absolutely not! This was not the only incident in which Mr. Swenson used his vehicle as a deadly weapon.

One day at dusk, my grandson, Brandon Ray was playing basketball with four of his friends across the street from my house. The ball had rolled onto the street and my grandson ran to get it. Mr. Swenson was headed North on the right lane with no headlights on. Brandon Ray was on the left lane waiting for Swenson to pass. Mr. Swenson decided to drive on the wrong side of the lane with his car headed directly at my grandson at the last second swerved his car to the right lane. Brandon and his friends ran immediately to tell me what had happened. I called the sheriff and filed a report. Was Mr. Swenson prosecuted for his attempt to threaten Brandon's life? Absolutely not!

Upon my insistence, the Washington County Sheriff's Department charged him with third degree assault, but I had to fight to get that. However the City of Lake St. Croix Beach refused to prosecute. When I was adamant that Mr. Swenson should be prosecuted, they sent the file to Richard Ilka, prosecutor for a sister City in Oakdale, MN. In my conversations with Mr. Ilka, he informed me that it would cost too much money to prosecute so they quashed the assault charge. When has the cost to prosecute ever been a consideration in dealing with an attempt to take someone's life, particularly when it's a child? There is no doubt in my mind that if the child were Caucasian, money would not be an object.

This is not the first time that Mr. Ilka was used for a whitewashing process to sanitize a wrongdoing. Mr. Ilka was also assigned the task of investigating the conduct of attorney Jon Erik Kingstad for his illegal conduct, when the St. Croix Villas Homeowner's Association accused him of misrepresentations and fraud. Once again Mr. Ilka found no wrong doing.

Evidence will show that Mr. Swenson repeatedly used his vehicle to terrorize and threaten anyone who supported me. One evening I was walking home from writing a purchase agreement on my neighbor's house just down the street from me, when suddenly I heard the sound of a vehicle behind me. I jumped to the curb to avoid getting run over and again it was Mr. Swenson driving with no headlights.

I tried to walk away from this uncivilized and corrupt valley, but the entire process was like stepping into a bog of slough and cesspool. The harder I tried to extricate myself the deeper it pulled me in. Like a cancerous growth that evolved from arrogance, hatred and contempt, these individuals who felt their power threatened wanted me wiped off the face of the earth for refusing to kow-tow to them and defending my principles. Standing up for what I thought was the right thing to do, ethically, morally and legally cost me everything that I have worked for my entire life. Was this my reward for daring to do the "right thing"? It was not my obligation to take a stand against those that wanted to preserve and protect a corrupt "status quo" that has existed for decades unchallenged in this "Valley of Evil". That obligation belongs to the state and federal enforcement agencies.

By this time I was a complete basket case with lawsuit after lawsuit designed to take my assets and seemingly no end in sight. It became clear that the Washington County District Court's judges were complicit

in this illegal process. My health was deteriorating to the point I could hardly function. I was being treated for severe depression, panic attacks, migraines, heart arrhythmia and a multitude of other stress—related ailments. I began to carry my nitroglycerin tablets on a locket around my neck as the problems became so severe. It was not unusual for me to get such severe panic attacks that I was taken by ambulance for emergency treatment because my blood pressure soared to 240 and upwards and I would pass out. I decided that I needed some protection from this onslaught of attacks for my personal safety.

Attempts to get an order for protection

I filed for an order for protection in early October, 2004, for my grandson and me and initially I was told that my order for protection was approved and that they would send it over to the Washington County Sheriff's Office to process. I waited for days and received no response, so I inquired again and I was told that I filled the form out incorrectly so I would have to start the process over. So again I completed the forms and when I called the next day, I was told to pick it up and take it to the Sheriff to process. I went to the Court Administrator, this time I was told that the judge wanted to see sheriff reports of the alleged attacks. I returned two days later (It took that long for the Sheriff's Office to process) and this time the excuse was that after two days, too much time had elapsed and I would have to start the process over again. Again, the third time I completed the forms and when I called the next day, I was told that the judge ordered a hearing and scheduled it for November 30th before Judge Schurrer. I appeared with a witness who witnessed one of the attacks by Bob Swenson.

Surprise! Surprise! There was no hearing even scheduled. When I went to the administrative clerk, I was told that there would be no hearing because Judge Hannon closed my case and that I could not file anymore orders for protection; if I insisted I would get an order for contempt. I asked for a copy of that order denying me protection, I was told that there was no written order only a verbal admonishment from the judge. I left and decided to have lunch and the more I thought about what had happened the angrier I got; as I realized I was being denied due judicial process and the perpetrator was being protected because of their connection with the City. I called attorney James Doran, and he told me that they cannot deny me a protection order when my life is being threatened and particularly that of my grandson who was a minor; and I should go back and make another request. I went back again and this time the head administrative clerk approached me. I very politely asked for another application and refused to leave until I received one. I called almost every day for over a week and there was always an excuse, i.e. "no judges to sign the order", or "it is still under advisement". A witness to this entire process made the determination that it couldn't be more obvious that "I have absolutely no rights" and it reminded her of the "Gestapo" when she lived in Nazi Germany.

On December 14, 2004, I called and again I spoke with Jennifer, Chief Administrative Clerk and I was told that Judge Muehlberg rejected the order for protection because there wasn't sufficient merit. I had attached to the application for protection, police reports filed on Swenson for his attempt to hit my grandson with his vehicle which was witnessed by several other children. I also attached police reports filed on my own behalf along with affidavits from third parties willing to testify that they witnessed Swenson coming at me head on with his car in a fit of rage. **And there is no merit? I have no way of knowing if indeed my applications for protection did go before any of the judges, since I was never given an opportunity to appear before one.**

Illegally Denied Voting Rights with Association

I had remained as Association President even when the project was sold to Michael Aymar. If the residents wanted me removed as President of the Association, all they had to do was call a meeting and remove me. That was the easy way. The City and its planners had to do things a little more dramatic because they didn't have the association vote to remove me. They used judges at Washington County to become involved with homeowner's meetings. In fact the City's planners, Parr and Swenson had ex parte communication with judges to facilitate my removal as president.

The Planners for the City eventually did take control of the Association but not without committing perjury by lying to the court appointed mediator. Therefore, essentially the court was used to remove me because there was not sufficient vote to do it legally. Since I still had four remaining pieces of property I should have had four votes. The following is a letter that I wrote to Tony Thooft.

July 12, 2005

St. Croix Villas Homeowner's Association
Attention: Mr. Tony Thooft, President
1375 Quasar Court
Lakeland, MN 55043

Dear Mr. Thooft:

It is my understanding that there will be another annual Association meeting to be held in July. It is also my understanding that notices have been sent to everyone with the exception of me. Let me make it very clear Mr. Thooft that if there is any intention of this Board (which consists of only you, since everyone has resigned) to block me from attending and voting as in the past by the previous Board, there will be significant consequences of which every homeowner could suffer from your decision to deprive me of my rights as a property owner.

I own three lots and I also own lot 13 with the dwelling in which title is essentially being argued in court. However, I still essentially have 4 votes. Records will reflect that I always paid my dues until I was denied services, so I consequently had to pay for lawn services myself. Also dues paid to the Association were used by the previous Board to illegal usurp funds to commence litigation against me. You have seen enough affidavits from other residents that indicate that it was the association that owed me $28,500. and not the reverse. You had plenty of opportunity as the President to correct this injustice, but you did nothing. So essentially what I see is that you are nothing more than an extension of the Parr and Swenson dictatorial regime. Now you tell me that I have no right to vote and you will call 911 if I show up to vote? Maybe you need to be named in the federal lawsuit as well for your illegal conduct?

What I find interesting is that if this is indeed now adjudicated as a senior housing, how is it that only the black family lost their home and all you white boys under 55 remain, which includes you with a son who was not 18? He may be an adult now, but for two years he was not.

I also for the record wish to state that your contempt for women was more than evident last night when you referred to Edith Ryan, Kay Smith and myself as "You f—king women" and "You three c—ksuckers". You should be ashamed of yourself, Mr. Thooft.

(signed by Marlene Fearing)

Edith Ryan and Kay Smith were also board members but resigned in protest for the way I was treated. When the meeting was held only Mr. Thooft remained as a board member and therefore, they had no legal quorum. Not to worry, because they brought in Dave Magnusson an attorney from Stillwater who was sitting in for Judge Maas to make sure I did not get to vote as an owner of four lots. I was told that if I appeared at the meeting and attempted to vote that they would call the sheriff and have me arrested. I appeared with attorney James Doran with my deeds to my property in hand as proof that I had four votes. We were told by attorney Dave Magnusson that my documents were void and we had to leave. There was no court order.

The following is only one of several letters that attorney James Doran wrote to the Association and a representative of the court, attorney Dave Magnusson. Mr. Doran made several phone calls and he received no return phone call or any response from any of the letters that he had written regarding my illegal eviction from the Homeowner's Association.

July 27, 2005

TO: Mr. Dave Magnusson (Sitting in for Judge Maas)
All Members of St. Croix Villas Homeowner's Assoc.

The undersigned represents Marlene Fearing and Progressive Real Estate, Inc. This letter is to advise you that the purported meeting of the homeowner's on July 22, 2005, was illegal for the following reasons:

1. *My client received no notice of the meeting as required under the by laws.*
2. *There was not a proper quorum under the by law rules. Therefore, all proxy votes were illegal as there was no Secretary of the Association serving at the time the proxies were given. Bylaws ARTICLE IV, Section 4. Quorum. "The presence at the meeting of members entitled to case, or of proxies entitled to cast, 60% of the votes of each class of membership shall constitute*

a quorum." Since five proxy votes do not count, there was no legal quorum.

3. *There was only one board member and the bylaws require that there must be three board members. ARTICLE V, Section 1. of the bylaws, "The affairs of the Association shall be managed by a Board of Directors. There shall be three (3) members of the Board of Directors. Clearly, this was a breach of fiduciary duty by Mr. Thooft, as president he had a duty to appoint and replace two members that resigned due to his refusal to conduct meetings. This is clearly willful and reckless conduct as was his role in allowing two members (Parr and Swenson) to sue other board members without taking any legal action to terminate their unlawful conduct and protect all members. The intent and purpose for the lawsuit (as records indicate) was purely a ruse to evict blacks. Mr. Thooft aided and abetted federal law to be violated by his refusal to act properly and timely. Mr. Thooft is only 46 years old and Mr. Thooft is aware that there are five others under the age of 55 whose home ownership was not terminated. Clearly, Mr. Thooft had knowledge that this was not a 55 and over project and he did absolutely nothing to protect members other than those bringing the litigation supposedly on behalf of the Association.*

4. *The Association and its state court appointed mediator deprived my client of her property rights under the 5th Amendment of the US Constitution by depriving her a right to vote as a member and as an owner of four lots. Progressive Real Estate is fee simple owner of lots 1, 2 and 3 and Marlene Fearing is owner of lot 13.*

Mr. Magnusson, even though you stated that my client was not a registered owner, clearly that was a misrepresentation because as of July 23, 2005 according to Washington County Recorder, Progressive is the owner in fee simple title. We are requesting a copy of the report that you relied on to deny my client her voting rights that would trump the certified copies of the deeds that we produced at the meeting. We're also requesting a new election.

My client feels that due to the role of this court appointed mediator that this is state sponsored discrimination and she is prepared to seek all legal remedies including but not limited to federal anti-discrimination laws. Given that this Board was not acting responsibly and pursuant to its own bylaws and its charter as a non-profit Corporation, my client will also seek damages against all members collectively and individually.

It's obvious to my client and me that this is ongoing retaliation against Ms. Fearing for her decision to defend a black family from eviction based on Judge Carlson's ruling. My client did her time and paid her fine for the contempt charge she received for simply writing a letter to the Association in defense of this black family. And for her role, she apparently has received a life sentence contempt order. Judge Carlson's ruling and adjudicating St. Croix Villas as a senior project was nothing more than a ruse to evict and discriminate against blacks. Case in point: This is now adjudicated 55 and older but yet none of the whites under 55 were evicted and in fact two are now appointed to the board. All of this was accomplished and approved under the eyes of the local judicial system. As the attorney involved in this project from the beginning, this was never a senior development. People of all ages lived at the Villas including those with children and that was never a problem until blacks arrived. Interestingly, Parr and Swenson as planners for the City and residents of the Villas lived there for seven years and never did they voice any objections regarding ages or children to my client, who was the President of the Association. Seven years later they sue under the guise of approval from the Association which was false and this Association did absolutely nothing to prevent or stop their action.

Sincerely,
James Doran, Attorney at Law.

Residents of the St. Croix Villas warned me of impending lawsuits being planned and coordinated by the City Planners and their Attorney to lay out a plan to have me incarcerated and to take all of my assets, including my home, my properties in Arizona and Mexico as well as my vehicles. This would all be accomplished with the aid of the Washington County Judicial System.

Excerpts from Affidavits of St. Croix Villa residents:

Edith Ryan—Dated July 9, 2003.

"I have been a resident of the St. Croix Villas for several years and I have witnessed the harassment of Marlene Fearing by the City and its agents Bob and Arlene Swenson and Mary Parr. *It appears that these attacks stem from the fact that she (Fearing) is also being blamed for Blacks moving in. It has been said that, 'Fearing wanted Blacks, and now she's got them.'"*

"I attended one meeting whereby Bob Swenson stated that he is going to 'get Fearing' if it's the last thing he does. Mary Parr made a similar comment about 'getting Fearing'. She indicated that she will spend her last nickel to 'get her' and then corrected by saying, well almost because she had the money to do it."

"When I inquired as to what Fearing ever did to her, Mary Parr indicated, '"She did nothing but she wanted Fearing's money."' I advised her to leave well enough alone because Fearing paid for street services for several years when the City refused to provide such services as street cleaning and snow and ice removal."

Diana Winters—Dated July 9, 2003

"I have been a resident of the Lake St. Croix Villas for several years and during that time I have observed ongoing harassment of Marlene Fearing by the City of Lake St. Croix Beach and depriving her of her ability to complete this project."

"At another meeting that I have attended which was organized by Bob and Arlene Swenson and Mary Parr, it's clear that they are receiving their direction from the City. There have been constant references made which implied that the City was very much involved in these attacks on Fearing."

"I noticed that since Marlene Fearing has returned from Arizona and that black people have taken up residency, the recent attacks on the project by the City have escalated."

"That Bob Swenson has made his racist views known when the black family first moved in the summer of 2002. *He immediately placed his home on the market, stating he wasn't going to live next door to a bunch* of "niggers". I informed Marlene Fearing of these comments and she was upset with me for repeating it."

Kathryn Smith—Dated on July 9, 2003

"I am the newest resident at the St. Croix Villas and I am simply appalled by the conduct of this City. They seem to have no regard for the law or the rights of property owners. Even though I have lived here a short time, I feel the harassment directed by this City toward the project and its original developer, Marlene Fearing has escalated recently".

"I have been solicited by Mary Parr and Arlene and Robert Swenson to join their efforts to sue Marlene Fearing. I am attacked and threatened with being served with legal documents for my refusal to participate in their litigation against Fearing. Mary Parr told me that I have no choice and that I will have enemies for not joining her and Bob and Arlene Swenson".

"As a property owner, I am very much concerned by this conduct because it is having a very negative effect on the values as well as the marketability of this property. I have heard from other residents that the motive behind this conduct is to depress the values of the property so they can be picked up at a very cheap price. It's real obvious to me that this effort is being organized and spear-headed by the City and Mary Parr and the Swensons".

"I intend to coordinate efforts with other homeowners to stop this greedy and mean-spirited conduct. If there is a common theme and goal that keeps surfacing it's the statements made by the Swenson's and Mary Parr, "'We're going to 'get her' (Fearing).'" While they attempt to 'get' Fearing, they're 'getting' the rest of us as well. Mary Parr stated that she will spend her last nickel to 'get' Fearing and then corrected herself by stating, well almost as she had the money to do it. This is illegal and wrong. *And what makes this even more obscene is that this effort to 'get' Fearing appears to be supported and directed by the City of Lake St. Croix Beach. It seems that everything is blamed on Fearing and the need to 'get' her for allowing Blacks to move in*".

"According to other residents at the villas, they have witnessed and observed this mean-spirited and outrageous conduct by the City and its agents directed at Marlene Fearing for years. They further indicated that they have felt helpless to intervene on Fearing's behalf for fear of retaliation by the City. They have witnessed that at times the City refused to clean or remove snow and ice from the streets and Fearing had to contract with private contractors to have that done. These are services that should be paid for by taxes being generated from taxpayers at this project and not by Fearing. My wish is that this childish behavior cease and we get this project back on track"

LITIGATION

In writing this documentary, I had to review thousands upon thousands of documents that were produced during the following lawsuits and it was like tearing open old wounds and living these horrors all over again. This process was not only extremely emotionally painful, laborious, but time intensive. It took me three years. After putting it down on paper and getting it all straight in my head, there is no doubt in my mind that all of this was a cleverly organized political scheme using the court system to retaliate against me and take my assets for the role I played in defending minorities. How to tell a story so full of hatred, venom and vengeance without sounding bitter and hateful myself was the challenge for me. I decided to take my Sister Salina's advise and "tell it just the way it is," because you cannot sugarcoat or paint a pretty picture from something this corrupt and evil.

I didn't know that human beings were capable of harboring such hatred for another human being, particularly when its government officials that's also the perpetrator. How can they be educated and still so ignorant? Just when I thought I had seen the worst despicable human behavior ever, I was surprised by yet another event even more shocking. To describe the events committed by those who would go to this extreme to keep their City "All White" is as difficult the second time around as from the first day I was exposed to it. In my entire life I have never witnessed anything so vile and sinister. To me, it's unbelievable that something like this can take place in the 21st Century, particularly America. This is behavior from the dark ages.

I have included much testimony from third parties of what they observed and witnessed. There are volumes of documents archived to display to anyone, because I discovered that much of my evidence that was presented to the courts was removed even though they appeared on the court roster as proof that they existed. In fact, entire files of mine, even those that were archived simply disappeared from the court files. I have repeatedly asked the court to investigate, but my requests were denied. Who took the documents and files? I do not know. I can only suspect that those who had the most to cover-up or gain from their absence would be the most likely individual or individuals.

In all of the following lawsuits, the "Rule of Law" and evidence were on my side, yet I could not get anything that resembled any fairness from any of these judges. They were all complicit in my peril. It was clear that the City's agents were given free rein to destroy me using unlawful tactics—fraud, misrepresentation, theft and perjury. Case in point: Mr. Kingstad was the attorney that fermented these lawsuits with the help of the City and their planners, Mary Parr and Robert Swenson. Mr. Kingstad became the instigator for such unlawful conduct with approval from every courtroom that he entered, including at the federal level. He was repeatedly rewarded attorney fees against me for his unlawful conduct in courtroom after courtroom even when he had no authority to represent these people in the role of Plaintiffs or Defendants. Mr. Kingstad had no authority to represent the Homeowner's Association as affidavits included will reveal, yet he continued with such false representation to the courts, claiming he was legal counsel when in fact, he was not. He used the Homeowner's Association as the catalyst to give him the necessary power to attack me. He could not get the support of other Homeowner's except for the City's Planners Mary Parr and Robert Swenson. Court after court he continued with his lies, while the Association members were helpless and essentially held hostage, because clearly this was government tyranny to maintain an "All White Society" with City Planners in the lead. In courtroom after courtroom Mr. Kingstad was rewarded with judgments against me for attorney fees when he had no jurisdiction or mandate to represent these people. But since he was a government stooge performing like a circus clown he had to be compensated somehow.

Excerpt from a letter to Mr. Kingstad, dated July 30, 2004.

"The lawsuit against Fearing was a personal lawsuit by Mary Parr and Robert Swenson, and neither initiated nor approved by the Association. We are in complete agreement, that any lis pendens should be dismissed voluntarily and not pursued further."

signed by the Homeowner's Association

Excerpt from a letter to Washington County Court, dated July 29, 2004.

"We wish to advise this court that this Association does not wish to pursue litigation against Fearing. We want this litigation ceased. While Mr. Kingstad is still representing that he is legal counsel, the truth of the matter is that he is not."

signed by the Homeowner's Association

Excerpt from a letter to Judge David Doyscher, dated Sept. 21, 2004.

"If Mr. Kingstad still continues to represent himself as legal counsel for the Association in matters pertaining to an ongoing legal battle between Parr/Swenson against Marlene Fearing, then he obviously is doing so against the expressed will of the Association and he has no legal authority to do so. For this and other reasons, several Association members have filed a complaint against Mr. Kingstad with the Office of Lawyers Professional Responsibility."

Excerpt from a letter to Judge Mary E. Hannon.

"We wish to advise this court that this Association does not wish to pursue litigation against Fearing and others. We want this litigation ceased. While Mr. Kingstad is still representing that he is legal counsel, the truth of the matter is that he is not."

Signed the Association Board.

Excerpt from a letter to Clerk of appellate Court, dated September 29, 2004.

"It has come to the attention of this Board that Mr. Jon Kingstad, legal counsel for Respondents (Mary Parr and Robert Swenson) is still representing that he is still legal counsel for this Association. *That is simply not the case.* Mr. Kingstad's representation was terminated simultaneously with the dismissal of Parr and Swenson as board members several months ago. Our new board is trying to correct some of the actions by the previous board and undo the damage it has caused to all homeowners and members of this Association."

signed by the Homeowner's Association

Note: *One would think that by now Mr. Kingstad would have gotten the message. Not so, the following excerpt is from another letter, written months later after he was told repeatedly to quit making false representations to the courts and to get lost.*

Excerpt from a letter to Chief Justice, Minnesota Court of Appeals.

"I attended a court hearing, whereby Mr. Kingstad stated under oath, that he represented the Homeowner's Association. *I knew that was not true."*

Signed by Secretary of Association, Kathryn Smith
January 5, 2005.

There were many more letters written privately to every judge from many members of the Association indicating that they did not want to be a part of this litigation. The court simply chose to turn a blind eye and pursue with their mandate to destroy Marlena Fearing.

When all is said and done, the "fall out" from all of this, caused by the perjury of Mr. Kingstad and his clients will no doubt tarnish the reputation of some judges at Washington District Court. The courts were told repeatedly that Mr. Kingstad had no authority to represent the Association, yet judge after judge allowed him to do so. I will give the benefit of a doubt and trust that some judges had 'no clue' as to what was transpiring. A couple of judges did recuse themselves from further participation when they finally figured out what was taking place, but the damage was already done. The two judges that disappointed me the most were Judge Doyscher and Judge Armstrong. I had the greatest respect and admiration for these two judges and I feel sorry that they chose to become part of this scam. Judge Hannon recused herself and as for Judge Maas, he was a dear sweet elderly gentleman that had no clue until the end when he refused to attend anymore so called 'Association meetings'. That's when Attorney Magnusson stepped in to take his place. There can be no doubt that the process was to vilify me through cooperative efforts by judges who acted as executioners rather than safe-keepers of the "Rule of Law".

Washington County District Court Lawsuits

LAWSUIT #1 and #2
File No. CX-96-3403 and C2-96-2830
Glenbrook Lumber, Featherstone Excavation
Colburn Carpentry and Buck Blacktop
Vs.
M.A. Fearing Companies, Inc. DBA River Valley Contractors

This was the first test case, so to speak, to test the waters for future such endeavors with judicial participation in destroying me, not only in terms of issues being litigated, but also establishing whether or not my legal representation would challenge any judicial improprieties. This was a mechanic lien case that was brought against me and the motives were clearly to extort monies from my Corporation that were not owed with the aid of the Washington County District Court. Judge John Cass was the presiding judge. This process was nothing short of a "gang bang" which Judge Cass participated in. This case proved fatal for my corporation because after the judgment was issued against me, my Corporation had to file for Bankruptcy.

The plaintiffs in this case were a collaboration by *a lumber company, a carpenter, a utilities contractor and a bituminous contractor* to illegally extort money from me that was not owed. All were friendly to the City.

The final result was that I received a judgment against me for approximately $195,000. I had no choice but to file for bankruptcy on behalf of my Corporation.

I believe that what transpired can be best told by the attorney that defended this case, James Doran.

Excerpts from Affidavit of James Doran, dated March 16, 2002

"I represented Ms. Fearing in the four mechanic lien cases. In each case, I verily believe that Ms. Fearing had a legitimate and principled defense. Unfortunately, all cases were assigned to Judge Cass. Judge Cass decided to consolidate all of the cases into one. I felt that was unfair and unreasonable for him to do so because each should have been heard

separately because each case was independent from the other and stood on their own facts."

"I verily believe that the Judge ignored crucial evidence that would have helped Ms. Fearing prevail in each case. In the case against the lumber company, evidence showed that thousands of dollars in material were not delivered, and wrong trusses were shipped and installed. It cost Ms. Fearing thousands of dollars to pay to have this corrected as best she could. Judge Cass ruled against Ms. Fearing and ordered her to pay attorney fees as well. *This act was contrary to any fairness and simple justice.*"

"In the matter of the carpentry, Ms. Fearing felt that her buyers should get good quality workmanship. She attempted to defend that principle and refused to pay for incompetence. One of her buyers testified that she could not open her refrigerator door because he had installed the cabinet incorrectly. She also testified that the front window was off center by almost three inches, the fireplace was installed in a crooked manner and trusses were installed backwards. Despite such evidence, Judge Cass ruled that the carpenter provided good workmanship. He ordered Ms. Fearing to pay the carpenter for his work and all of his attorney fees. *Again this ruling was contrary to any fairness and simple justice.*"

"In the case of the utility contractor, records showed that Ms. Fearing had actually overpaid him by $1,500. In court, the contractor admitted that he had a bookkeeping problem. Nevertheless, Judge Cass ignored the evidence of the overpayment and ordered Ms. Fearing to not only pay him again, but to pay his attorney fees as well. *I repeat, this act was contrary to any fairness and simple justice.*"

"In the matter of the bituminous company, Ms. Fearing did pay a majority of the bill, but withheld a portion until the City accepted their work. I felt both the contractor and Ms. Fearing were victims of the City's misconduct. The City Engineer, SEH determined the plans and specifications (Outlined in the Development Agreement) for the road, including the curbs and driveway. Ms. Fearing's engineer (Nyhus Engineering) drew them accordingly with SEH's approval. The City engineer would not accept the road even though it was constructed to their specifications. (It was a catch 22) Judge Cass didn't seem to be interested in the conduct of the City and ruled in the contractors favor and ordered that the remainder of the bill be paid as well as the contractor's attorney fees. One buyer couldn't drive in or out of her driveway because of the surmountable curb that SEH required the contractor to install, but Judge Cass ruled it was good workmanship. (Interesting Note: Ms. Fearing paid to correct the curbing, but made no correction to the road itself. Once the judgment was made against Ms. Fearing, the City didn't seem to have a problem with the road and accepted it as installed.)"

"Overall, I vehemently disagree with the rulings of Judge Cass. I don't believe he considered any favorable evidence for Ms. Fearing in any of these cases. Had he done so, Ms. Fearing would have received the offsets she deserved in these cases. In addition, had she received these offsets, I don't think Ms. Fearing would have had to pay their attorney fees. Ms. Fearing instructed your affiant prior to trial to negotiate in good faith the claims submitted by each mechanic's lien plaintiff, but to no avail. All monies had been escrowed in advance at Universal Title Company."

"It is Ms. Fearing's belief that her clients should receive good quality workmanship. In all of these cases, your affiant believes Ms. Fearing's position was right and justified."

"In hindsight, Ms. Fearing should have filed against Judge Cass particularly after an incident that occurred at an initial hearing which was held in a county boardroom while the courtroom was being remodeled. *Judge Cass, in my presence, requested Ms. Fearing step into a private area away from the hearing room. When Ms. Fearing returned, I asked her what was that all about? Ms. Fearing indicated that Judge Cass asked her all kinds of personal questions and then told her that she reminded him of his ex-wife. I asked Ms. Fearing if that was a good sign? Needless to say, I thought the conduct of Judge Cass was a little bizarre to say the least.*"

Given the fact that I had to escrow monies in advance of the findings is quite revealing in that, the outcome was already known before the case was tried. How else would the plaintiff's attorneys know how much money to request for escrow in advance—to the exact penney? This was not the first time in Washington County District Court where I was the defendant that predetermined court results were known in advance of any court hearings.

*   *   *

LAWSUIT # 3
File No. CO-03-3415
Parr/Swenson St. Croix Villas Homeowner's Assoc., et al.
vs
Fearing, Perlinger, et al.

This lawsuit was designed to evict blacks and retaliate against me for defending them. Sixty eight pages of evidence disappeared, all supporting my position and I was jailed for refusing to evict blacks. At the time the lawsuit was initiated against me, I was still the President of the Association. Attorney Kingstad nor the City's Planners, Mary Parr and Robert Swenson had any legal authority to initiate this lawsuit. Yet they submitted fraudulent affidavits falsely claiming they represented the Association.

- This action was brought against me by (Mary Parr and Bob Swenson) two Planners for the City of Lake St. Croix Beach. According to local residents who lived at the "Villas" this lawsuit was being fermented by The City of Lake St. Croix through their attorneys and Jon Erik Kingstad, the attorney representing the City planners, Parr and the Swensons. They alleged that I fraudulently misrepresented the project to be a senior development. **City Planners, Parr and Swenson lived at the project for seven years during the time that people of all ages lived there, even those with children. Ages of residents and children only became an issue when a white couple moved in with several black children.** The Statue of Limitation should have precluded Parr and Swenson from bringing any action because this lawsuit was filed a year too late. This case was originally assigned to Judge Mary Carlson, who acknowledged in open court that she was aware that it was the City that was behind this action when she made the following comment in open court, **"I do not want to hear anything about discrimination because this City is too small". The City was not the plaintiff in this matter, but clearly this judge knew it was the City's lawsuit. After that outburst, she calls for a meeting in the privacy of her chambers with all legal counsel.**
- Behind closed doors Judge Carlson admitted to Attorney Mark Kallenbach that, "she did not much care for his client, Marlena Fearing". I found that interesting, since I had never met the woman

nor have I ever appeared before her in court. I believe a fair and honest Judge would have recused herself if she had such a predisposed affliction, but from her findings it was clear she had a mission to assist in the destruction of Marlena Fearing. Also in her findings, she reveals information only known to the City and was never a matter of court record. In fact some language is almost identical to information provided to the U.S. Justice Investigator which was written by the City when their funds were frozen by U.S. Justice Department. That begs the question then as to who wrote Judge Carlson's Findings in this case if this evidence was not entered into court record?

- When this lawsuit was initiated against me, Mr. Kingstad, attorney supposedly representing the Homeowner's Association had no such mandate from the Association. His clients were not even members of good standing and he in no way had such authority. Several homeowners wrote to the judge indicating that they did not want this lawsuit to move forward and that City Planners and their attorney Kingstad had no authority to commence such a lawsuit. This was a complete fraud upon the court and the court ignored all protests from Association members. Neither attorney supposedly defending me in this case, Mr. Kallenbach and Mr. Lemmons raised any of these issues before the judge.

- Affidavits of residents indicated that the St. Croix Villas was never a senior development and that the Homeowner's Association owed me $28,500, which was also supported by numerous affidavits. Yet, Judge Carlson ruled against me in spite of such evidence. I felt that their was a pattern here of judicial misconduct, whereby any evidence favorable to me was ignored or magically disappears from the file, therefore, I am denied due judicial process even at the appellate level. When evidence and the law were on my side, Judge Carlson in her findings increased the ages of the residents and declared the "Villas" a senior community and awarded ridiculous judgments against me—$23,000 to the Association and $33,000. in attorney fees. Attorney Kingstad, who represented the City planners was essentially rewarded for committing perjury and a fraud upon the court and evidence supports this allegation.

- During the court proceedings, Mr. Kingstad, attorney for the City's agents asked the judge to have me incarcerated and to keep me in jail until I release all of my properties to them and then he wanted me ordered out of town for good. Everyone in the courtroom was

shocked that anybody could even make such a request. What did my
attorney Kallenbach do? Absolutely nothing. He stood and looked on
in a daze. He also seemed in shock, but he said nothing in my defense.

- As President of the Association I had a duty and an obligation to
protect the integrity of the Association. When the racist views of
both Parr and Swenson became known when they attempted to evict
the black family, I wrote a letter to the Association in protest of their
eviction because I knew it was racially motivated. In my attempt to
uphold federal and state housing laws, I was made the "scape goat"
for what I perceive to be State sanctioned discriminatory efforts with
full cooperation and acquiescence of the judicial system.

- **This entire case was merely a ruse to evict the blacks by this City
and its planners, Parr and Swenson. A process that was further
sanctioned and facilitated by Judge Mary Carlson.** If this is indeed
adjudicated as a senior housing, why is it that only the blacks were
evicted by the association even though they owned their home? All the
whites under 55 did not get evicted and in fact, they received "Special
Mandates" to remain at the project. Since Judge Carlson adjudicated
the project as 55; several more whites have taken up residency all
under 55. This is further evidence that the age 55 contentions was
not only an excuse to evict the blacks, but to also harm me financially
with the judgments awarded to Parr and Swenson by Judge Carlson.
**Interesting note: I was sued because I sold to people under 55
but now since the ruling of Judge Carlson rendering the Villas
a senior housing, they are allowing people under 55 to take up
residency in violation of the supposed court order. However, since
they are all white folks, there is no problem.**

- When I requested an investigation as to why I was denied a right
to vote at the Homeowner's Association when there was no court
order denying such a vote, that request was also denied. I also got no
response from the court, when I inquired as to how City planners,
Mary Parr and Arlene Swenson are privileged to ex parte phone
conversations with retired Judge Maas. Judge Maas subsequently
appointed Attorney Magnuson to substitute for him as a court
appointed mediator to attend a meeting and once again deny me a
right to vote. (This conversation was witnessed by a neighbor) This
is clearly a violation of my constitutional rights, all being conducted
under the "Color of the Law". **I found it interesting that in every
case that came before the court, my neighbors informed me of the**

findings months in advance as to the outcome. In other words, findings were established before any evidence was admitted to the court. It appears that City Hall renders the decisions as to how much to punish me financially and the process is rubber stamped by judges friendly to City Hall.

- This is the same State sanctioned discrimination that my attorney, James Doran complained about in his letter to a court appointed mediator (David Magnusson) when he illegally blocked my right to vote at the Association meeting to elect new officers. There was no court order to deny me a vote, yet the court aided in efforts to deny me my Constitutional rights to a vote as a homeowner. (Doran Letter is in "Illegally Denied Voting Rights" section)
- I was first warned by Judge Carlson that I could not speak with my neighbors (clearly a violation of my first amendment rights) and then found in contempt of court by Judge Mary Hannon for writing the letter for which I received a fine or 30 days in Jail (Again a violation of my first amendment rights). However, since Judge Hannon subsequently recused herself when I made it known that I would not pay a fine to defend the Constitution, the file was assigned to Judge Armstrong.

Letter written by members of Association to Judge Mary Carlson

November 19, 2003
Honorable Judge Mary Carlson
Dear Judge Carlson:

We the undersigned respectfully request that you give consideration to calling for a new election of Board of Directors at the St. Croix Villas or completely dissolving the Association. We know that you worked extremely hard at getting a mediator to fairly elect a new Board of Directors. Unfortunately, there was no resemblance to fairness, not to mention a violation of our basic rights, when some members are so desperate for control that they chose to lie to Judge Maas about their status with the Association. It was decided that only those who were current in their association dues could vote. The problem with that is this: Mary Parr, Bob and Arlene Swenson and Phyllis Riley told Judge Maas that they were current with their dues, when in fact they were not, and records reflect this. Swenson's in particular had huge assessments against them for violations much greater than those assessed against any of us. Yet they

were rewarded for their dishonesty, while those of us that admitted we were not current with our dues were punished for our honesty. The only fair thing to do would have been to allow all owners a vote regardless of the dues and assessment issue. Many of us tried to join when Mary Parr was Secretary-Treasurer under the previous board, however, Mary Parr, at the time denied us services at the same time preventing some of us from joining. That is why many of us refused to pay for services we were denied and the reason that Mary Parr was eventually removed from the board by other board members. Now that Parr is back in power, we essentially live under a tyranny. We understand that there are rules and regulations to follow under an Association, but we should not have to live under an environment, whereby we feel threatened and see our properties being devalued by the conduct of the present board. It appears that we have no rights at all and live essentially under a "Dictatorship".

The following are just a few of the transgressions against us by the present board.

1. Both Parr and the Swenson's on numerous occasions have trespassed and harassed any new potential buyers with their negative propaganda about the development and discouraging anyone from buying here. They peak into windows to observe who the occupants are and how many. (Attached Sheriff reports will confirm this)

2. Parr called a meeting to determine what to do about one family who has children. Even though it was slated as a meeting, Ms. Parr chose to call it a Hearing, thereby, stating that in a Hearing nobody got to speak except her. The allegations against this particular family by the present board is not only that they have children, but too many of them as well. When one member inquired as to why there is opposition to children when children were allowed in the project previously and nobody complained then. But now that the children are black there is a claim that children aren't allowed. If any one attempted to address the unfairness of this meeting, they were threatened with eviction by the sheriff. In fact some did leave because of the threats. At the end of the meeting the board passed out a survey containing questions that clearly were in violation of our basic constitutional rights. Many of us that attended that meeting felt that this was racially motivated. (A tape of the meeting is available for verification) An added note of interest that should be given consideration is this. Not only has

this present board attempted to remove this family with children by claims of "No Children" allowed in this project, but at the same time two board members have filed a complaint against this family with Washington County Child Protection, falsely claiming that they are abusing their children. So it appears the effort is to get rid of them by any means possible. The racist comments that are floating about by this present board supports that contention.

3. Those of us that bought from the original developer were never told that this would be a "Senior Only" project. We were told it was designed for empty nesters and retirees, with no representation of restrictions such as age or children. There were no special provisions that would legally permit this development from these kind of exemptions. When a subsequent developer took over the project, they received approval from the City of Lake St. Croix Beach to change the design from a 2 bedroom to a 3 bedroom. With Parr and Swenson on the planning board for the City, they obviously had knowledge and gave their support of this change. They were also responsible for changing this project into a family project and now they claim it's for seniors and no children are allowed. The make up presently of the residents are 50% under the age of 55 and 50% above 55.

Please give our request serious consideration, Judge. Many of us purchased here because of the apparent peaceful and tranquil environment only to find that the conditions surrounding the present board and the Association are barely tolerable. We want to live in some peace and harmony, but see no prospect of that with the ongoing harassment by this present board. We also see no real possibility for change unless the restrictive bylaws which have become meaningless (There is no common area—a zero lot line concept) and in our opinion can only be accomplished by the dissolution of the Association.

Sincerely,

Members of The Lake St. Croix Villas Homeowner's Association
Signature page sent to Judge Carlson

Evidence shows that Parr, Swenson and their attorney Jon Eric Kingstad committed perjury and a fraud upon the court, as outlined in my Rule 11 Motion, which I filed with the court only to find it rejected, not once, but twice. It was obvious the court did not want the truth as to what was taking place so the evidence was removed. My affidavit with supporting evidence which I submitted to the court outlined in detail the perjury and fraud committed by Parr, Swenson and their Attorney Jon Kingstad, yet all that evidence was removed from the file. The following is a motion that I filed with the court, which cost me a filing fee. They took my filing fee but I was denied use of the court room to argue my motion.

*   *   *

STATE OF MINNESOTA	DISTRICT COURT
COUNTY OF WASHINGTON	TENTH JUDICIAL DISTRICT

MARY PARR, ROBERT SWENSON AND ARLENE SWENSON, et al in their personal capacity and as members and representatives of LAKE ST CROIX VILLAS HOMEOWNERS ASSOCIATION, a Minnesota nonprofit corporation,	Court File No. CO-03-3415
Plaintiffs,	Defendant's Request for A Re-Hearing for Rule 11 Sanctions Against Plaintiffs and their attorney, JonErik Kingstad.
v.	
MARLENE FEARING, Progressive Real Estate, Inc. et al. Defendants.	

PLEASE BE ADVISED that on February 27, 2006 at 9:a.m. or as soon, thereafter, that Judge Thomas Armstrong, presiding judge in this matter may hear this motion in Washington County Government Center, 14949—62nd Street North, Stillwater, Minnesota 55082, the Defendant in this matter will move the Court for the following:

1. In a recent court hearing Defendant Fearing, appeared Pro se and requested a rehearing of the Rule 11 Motion, due to newly discovered evidence. Judge Armstrong indicated verbally that Defendant Fearing would be granted another Hearing.
2. Judge Armstrong's earlier finding was that the Plaintiff's had not received sufficient notice and offenses were not articulated.
3. It appears that according to correspondence from my prior legal counsel, Mark Kallenbach, the issue of bringing a Motion for a Rule 11 was addressed on several occasions due to the same complaints I have with the Plaintiffs and their legal counsel, Jon Erik Kingstad, offering perjured testimony, false and fraudulent claims to the court.
4. Plaintiffs had sufficient warning and time to clean up their act.
5. This motion is supported by the affidavits, letters and exhibits attached, hereto.

Respectfully Submitted,

Marlene Fearing, Attorney Pro se

(I attached the 68 pages of documents that were removed from the file)

* * *

While Judge Armstrong claimed at sentencing that he had no alternative but to sentence me for 30 days, I wholeheartedly disagreed. That was a further violation of my First Amendment Rights. I refused to pay the fine as a protest of such flagrant violations of my basic Constitutional Rights. For Judge Armstrong to blindly accept what was predisposed by a previous judge who may have had ulterior motives or prejudices seems to be the problem that exists in Washington County District Court. Clearly there was mounting evidence that the local State court instead of upholding the laws of this Nation were rewriting the Constitution from the bench. That is the function of Congress, not the courts. There exists a real systemic problem in Washington District Court pertaining to Constitutional issues.

At sentencing Judge Armstrong tells me a story about his Norwegian friend who was very stubborn and didn't want to remove illegal waste from his property, but he finally saw the light and removed it. He goes on to tell me that I should see the "light". After a long pause he asks me for a comment. I responded as follows:

> *"Your Honor I see the light and it sure is not the Beacon for Democracy and Freedom. My first amendment rights are being violated as I had every right to write that letter, particularly in defense of the illegal conduct initiated by the Plaintiffs in this matter against black homeowners. I will not pay a fine to defend the Constitution and there comes a time when one must stand up and defend their principles, otherwise, why have any? On two separate occasions I filed a Rule 11 Motion against Mr. Kingstad for his perjury and fraudulent conduct in this case, which my attorneys, Kallenbach and Lemmons neglected to do. You declined to hear those motions. You also declined my request to investigate the disappearance of 68 pages of my supporting documents in this case. Now I am being jailed for doing the "right thing", ethically, morally and legally, while Mr. Kingstad and his clients, who have repeatedly committed fraud and perjury are rewarded for their conduct by assessing judgments against me for attorney fees. The way I see it, we ought not send our troops off to wars to die for supposed democracy and freedoms that do not exist here at home".*

At the time that I filed for an appeal of Judge Carlson's findings to the State Appellate Court, I discovered that evidence (affidavits and other supporting documents) in support of my case disappeared from my file, 68 pages to be exact. When an Officer of the Homeowner's Association, Kaye Smith, attempted to deliver these missing documents to the appellate court, they were refused as they were not part of the record, however they were listed on the court roster as being filed. Clearly, an interesting phenomenon. Subsequently, additional files of mine took on a missing status, even those that were archived. I am not to suspect that something is amiss? If this was for the purpose of editing my files, I will never know, but such action further supports my allegations of improprieties. There were many witnesses to verify what transpired in the court room, who were as shocked as I was to witness such mockery of the judicial process. When I asked the court for an investigation as to what was transpiring with my files, that request was denied. If there were no shenanigans taking place, why did my files disappear?

Once again the blind eye of the court denied me fair judicial process and facilitated the plaintiff's in their fraudulent conduct. When documents supporting my allegations are removed from my files and I am not given an opportunity to address the court, I suspect unclean hands by judges as well. I view this not only as efforts to redefine Marlena Fearing, but a redefining of the Constitutional Bill of Rights. This is perhaps how the judicial system works in North Korea or China, but this is America and we don't do things that way here, or do we?

It became obvious to me that the judicial process in Washington County District Court became an extension of City Hall and a mandate existed to aid in the destruction of Marlena Fearing by denying me my basic constitutional rights. Regardless of how the court wants to define me, under the "color of the law", my rights have been repeatedly violated with the aid of the court, I am still an American and as such entitled to due process. While I was held in contempt by the court, it is the court that is in contempt—contempt of due judicial process and governing laws and statutes. There are too many inexplicable phenomenon taking place at the courts that suggests criminal intent by complicity in suborning perjury and fraud and rewarding attorney Kingstad judgments against me. Attorney Jon Erik Kingstad did not have authority by the Association to even initiate this lawsuit. Affidavits and letters from Villa residents clearly show that he had been removed. And yet Mr. Kingstad continued to represent the Association at the Minnesota Appellate court, where he was rewarded with more attorney fees, and then to the Minnesota Supreme court and the U.S. Supreme court. The Minnesota Appellate court knew that he had no authority to represent the Association and the court also knew that 68 pages were removed from the file and yet they rewarded Mr. Kingstad more attorney fees. And we call this JUSTICE?

The following are excerpts from affidavits from some residents of the Villas.

Affidavit of Edith Ryan, dated October 8, 2004.

"I have lived at the St. Croix Villas Development since 1998, and people of all ages have resided here even those with children. This was never marketed or existed as a 55 plus community."

Affidavit of Jimmy Hahn, dated October 1, 2004

"I have resided at St. Croix Villas since June 1, 2003. I am the oldest resident residing at my home and *I am 28 years old*. During my residency, at no time has the Association provided services for the physical or social needs of older persons, nor has the Association ever made available any amenities or facilities for older persons.

During my residency, the Association has never published or provided any written materials to me which would indicate that the Association intended that it be occupied only by persons 55 years of age or older".

Affidavit of Diane Winters, dated October 9, 2004

"I have lived at the St. Croix Villas Development since 1998, and people of all ages have resided here even those with children. This was never a 55 plus community.

I attended an Association meeting whereby all future fees on vacant lots were waived for Ms. Fearing in exchange for her forgiving debt owed to her by the Association in the amount of approximately $28,000."

Affidavit of Theodor Perlinger, dated October 1, 2004

"I have lived at the St. Croix Villas Development since 1995 and this development was never sold to me as a 55 plus community. Over the years, people of all ages have resided here even those with children.

I attended an Association meeting whereby all future fees on vacant lots were waived for Ms. Fearing in exchange for her forgiving debt owed to her by the Association in the amount of more than $28,000. Therefore, the bank account of the Association was opened with a zero balance.

That Mary Parr or Mr. Kingstad failed to produce the records of this agreement to the court either purposely or unintentionally during the court proceedings I attended."

In spite of that evidence, Judge Mary Carlson awarded them $23,000 for Association fees and $33,000. in attorney fees for bringing this bogus lawsuit against me. In her findings she also increased the ages of the residents from what they stated under oath in their affidavits and adjudicated the project as "senior only". Never mind that the project meets no HOP or HOPA guidelines or State or Federal Housing guidelines—we have a State district court judge with more power than the federal courts, including the Supreme Court.

*   *   *

LAWSUITS #4 and #5—Involving City's chosen Developer Mr. Aymar
 # 82-C5-03-005435 and 82-C7-03-0005131
Michael Aymar
Vs. Marlene Fearing
Foreclosure—Quiet Title Action

Mr. Aymar sued me twice, first for specific performance on a purchase agreement on my land that I refused to close on when I found out from U.S. Justice Department (Under Clinton) that the City had decided to orchestrate this sale. The second lawsuit that Aymar brought against me was to cancel the original contract that he sued me to enforce. When Aymar initiated his second lawsuit against me in an unlawful detainer action, he was in default of our contract and had not made a payment in over a year. He defaulted and then laid blame on me and sued me, at the same time he was trying to evict me from my original home that I had built.

(Now enters attorney Chad Lemmons) Mr. Aymar didn't show up in court and we won a default judgment against Aymar for almost $600,000. For whatever reason, only Attorney Lemmons knows the answer, but he failed to file or docket the $600,000. judgment. His negligence essentially allowed Mr. Aymar to subsequently place more fraudulent mortgages against my remaining lots. When I discovered that the judgment had not been recorded, I had it docketed however, it was too late because the mortgages taken by Mr. Aymar became senior in position which left me with no equity since Mr. Aymar stripped all the equity. The question now becomes whose interest was Mr. Lemmons representing here—certainly not mine, since his negligence cleared the way for Aymar to steal my property.

*   *   *

LAWSUIT # 6
UNITED STATES BANKRUPTCY COURT
Case # BKY 03-46682
Michael Aymar

In Mr. Aymar's initial bankruptcy filing he told the court that he had virtually no income, no assets, no real estate holdings and all that he owned was his car and the clothes on his back. At the creditors meeting, however, he stated that he actually made about $30,000 a year, and paid $3,000. per month in child support. The Trustee obviously wasn't interested in questioning Mr. Aymar on his calculations because if indeed he paid $3,000 in child support, he was paying out more than he was earning.

Mr. Aymar also didn't acknowledge the fact that he had recently deeded a house that he owned to his ex-wife and that he owned a yacht docked on the St. Croix River. He also did not disclose that he had money in several bank accounts that he withdrew just before filing for bankruptcy.

I requested a deposition of Mr. Aymar so he could explain to the court how he could possibly file for bankruptcy when he had just earned in excess of $1,000,000. by flipping properties which he was not disclosing to the court. I sold my lots to Mr. Aymar at a price of $41,000. per lot. He immediately placed mortgages on eight (approximately $300.000 on each) of them to construct the town homes. He then withdrew $95,000. per each lot thus pocketing the money on property in some cases still owned by me. In other words, he stripped all value from the property. This thievery was sanctioned by the City of Lake St. Croix Beach, the Washington County District Court and subsequently the Federal Court as well. The value more than doubled because lots had a much greater value when the City agreed to give Mr. Aymar building permits which they weren't willing to give to me.

I sold my property to Mr. Aymar under a Contract for Deed which the Real Estate Closer and Title Company (First Advantage Title) did not record. This enabled Mr. Aymar to mortgage my property illegally and pocket the proceeds. Mr. Aymar with the help of the Title Company and Mr. Thomas Whiteis, its president pocketed in excess of $1,000,000. and then Mr. Aymar filed for bankruptcy. On further examination Mr. Aymar acknowledges that he also hadn't filed income taxes for eight years personally or on his businesses. How outrageous is that? Both Mr. Aymar and Mr. Tom Whiteis are licensed by the State of Minnesota. In other words, they carry licenses to steal from the public and the State of Minnesota does absolutely nothing to protect the public from such thievery.

At the deposition, Mr. Aymar finally acknowledges an income of $150,000. (My investigators reported more than double that amount $200,000-$300,000. flowing through the various bank accounts). Mr. Aymar admitted to the trustee that he didn't declare it because he did not want to pay off any debts to the creditors (mainly my corporation and me personally). My attorney, Mark Kallenbach sat through these proceedings and later commented to me that he felt Mr. Aymar needed a good criminal attorney especially after acknowledging that he had not only committed perjury, but acknowledged that he was engaging in bankruptcy fraud and tax evasion. This is just another example of Mr. Kallenbach's inability to protect me, by refusing to file any motions with the court to have Mr. Aymar held in contempt for bankruptcy fraud.

I was certain that minimally Mr. Aymar's petition for bankruptcy would be disallowed, but then for the court to allow him to escape unscathed from these proceedings after he committed bankruptcy fraud, admitted to tax fraud and perjured himself under oath, was just too much for me to comprehend.

From information gathered by my investigators, GNA, from the Washington County Recorder's office and court documents, it appears that Mr. Aymar worked under the name of various corporations, i.e. Transaction Real Estate, Pro-Action Mortgage, First Advantage Title, LSCB,LLC, Property Holdings and other straw buyers to conceal his money laundering through various land purchases and property flipping schemes.

The benefit to Mr. Aymar is that even though these are shell corporations once filed they can get a checking account number and operate as a legal entity. So even though they do no business they seem to be funded and can write personal checks and hide under the corporate veil.

There are a number of companies that all operate out of the same address. According to information gathered by my investigators, the

Aymars operate a real estate sales company, a mortgage company and an appraisal company. They also seem to pay their agents from any number of companies. Illegal as hell, but it appears that neither the State of Minnesota nor the U.S. Bankruptcy Court could give a damn because they certainly were made aware of what was transpiring. I don't have a degree in law and if I can figure this one out, why can't the authorities?

Transaction Real Estate was the company used to purchase my land and then the contract was assigned to LSCB, LLC. Supposedly Transaction Real Estate is owned by Brother Marc Aymar even though MN statues require that the broker must be an officer of the corporation. Records show that Michael Aymar is listed as broker of record. However, in 2003 brother Marc Aymar went into court and testified that his brother Michael Aymar had nothing to do with this company. Michael is, however, listed as broker and officer of record of the corporation at the State Commerce Licensing Division in Minnesota. His brother was listed as president. This can only mean then that Brother Marc and Michael himself lied to the courts even when this information was evidenced by public record. That is called perjury, but again no harm comes to Mr. Aymar.

Another company that was operating out of the same address by the Aymar Brothers is called Pro Action Mortgage. This company is in another brother's name, David Aymar, but this company is frequently used to pay the agents working for Transaction Real Estate, even though this corporation had no listed agents in 2003. How can a company with no agents pay agents licensed under another corporate entity?

One Aymar brother (Marc) informed my investigators that they made their agents incorporate and in doing so the money was constantly running from one corporation to another. This is how Michael Aymar pays no federal or state taxes. It's no surprise then that some of the properties were traded according to the Washington County Recorders office five times in a matter of days.

All of the above information was provided to the Bankruptcy Trustee, Mr. Leonard to show that Mr. Aymar was indeed committing a fraud against the U.S. Bankruptcy Court. In spite of all of this evidence, Mr. Leonard not only granted Mr. Aymar a bankruptcy discharge but also allowed him to remain in title of my land under a contract for deed that should have been quashed and land returned to me as the rightful owner. This trustee has a lot of explaining to do for his conduct in this matter. Nobody can possibly be that stupid particularly when placed in such a powerful position. Mr. Leonard, a U.S. Bankruptcy Trustee, virtually aided Mr. Aymar in defrauding me in excess of one and a half million dollars by allowing his bankruptcy when evidence of fraud couldn't be more apparent.

This begs the question, how can someone this incompetent, this lazy and this stupid remain on federal payroll funded by our tax dollars?

There was another report (9 pages) which was written by another creditor by the name of Robert Nuis. His report reflects and confirms all of my allegations and would be redundant to repeat here. He submitted his report to the bankruptcy court which has now become a matter of public record. Much of his information was taken from public record and documentation supplied by my investigators which he submitted to the bankruptcy court. This is further evidence of the extent of the fraud and perjury committed by Mr. Aymar and his accomplices involving my property. The following are a few excerpts from that report by Mr.Nuis, aptly named, "Bankruptcy for Profit":

"Bankruptcy for Profit"—Written by Robert Nuis

I have contacted the trustee (Mr. Brian Leonard) on three separate occasions concerning Mr. Aymar's acknowledgement that his purpose for filing bankruptcy was to defraud creditors. In all cases, Mr. Leonard has failed to respond to any of my correspondence. Failure by the system to have this individual prosecuted for bankruptcy fraud is the true crime. Allowing this individual to slip through the hands of Justice repeatedly and abuse a system that essentially was established to protect the public shows a definite flaw in the bankruptcy judicial system.

My last letter to him was to confirm what has been done, but again I received no response from him and can only assume from his lack of response that nothing has been done. I became a bit confused when I ran the last name "Aymar" on the bankruptcy records and discovered that there had been five (5) bankruptcies filed under this last name (Aymar) in the last 10 years, four (4) of those were chapter 7's and of those four (4) bankruptcies, Brian F. Leonard was the trustee for three (3) of them. You would think that someone might spot a pattern here. By the way, his attorney was paid by a check from AAABCD Corporation, another company not listed by Michael and it was amazing we could only find his name on the checking account, something else that triggered no reaction in his attorney or from the trustee. This should have set off an alarm for her, but since this is the second bankruptcy she has done for him it was apparently too much trouble to look into it.

*   *   *

LAWSUIT # 7

UNITED STATES BANKRUPTCY COURT

CASE # BKY: 06-32591
Attorney Jon Erik Kingstad, attorney
Mary Parr, Bob and Arlene Swenson
Vs.
PROGRESSIVE REAL ESTATE, INC
Once again, government stooge Jon Erik Kingstad is engaging in yet another "Freak Show". Under oath and penalty of perjury, Mr. Kingstad and his clients falsely allege that my corporation owes them $414,000. by filing a Involuntary Bankruptcy claim against my corporation that has been non existent since 1998. The only asset owned by my corporation was undeveloped land at the Villas Project, and they want to lay claim to that land as well. This is clearly another fraud and the U.S. Bankruptcy Trustee is equally complicit in allowing it. This is the second case in which the U.S. Justice Department is complicit in aiding another land grab of my property. The first case was the City's chosen developer, Mike Aymar and this time it is the City's Planners and their attorney Jon Erik Kingstad.

I consulted with several bankruptcy attorneys, and I was told that I need not have an attorney present to represent the corporation because *if there was no evidence or proof of such a judgment and none provided to the court, then the court must dismiss this case as **"a matter of law"**.*

I notified the court that not only did I not receive any notice of the Involuntary Bankruptcy filing but it was untimely when I did receive it, therefore, I could not respond timely. (This is what is so typical and predictable of Mr. Kingstad's conduct. He submits an affidavit to the court attesting to certified mailing to me, when in fact it was not even filed timely.) When I put in an answer to the court, they rejected it as untimely and by that time, the court had already granted Mr. Kingstad and the City Planners the involuntary bankruptcy claim. This kind of behavior is prevalent by Mr. Kingstad throughout all litigation involving him which has also been repeatedly pointed out to the courts. My complaints have been repeatedly ignored by the court and favor paid to Mr. Kingstad. Once again what we have here is a federal court suborning perjury, and allowing this fraud to continue.

Excerpts from a letter I wrote to bankruptcy trustee John Hedback, dated February 15, 2008.

Letter to Trustee:

Dear Mr. Hedback:

I am writing in response to our conversation of last week which I find quite troubling given your position, that "I had my day in court". How did I have my day in court when I have been denied due process as 100% owner of corporate stock and creditor of Progressive Real Estate, Inc? For court record, I wish to state all of the following:

If I had my day in court then you are suborning Plaintiff's fraud and perjury in this matter. There is no judgment against me in the amount of $414,000. I have repeatedly asked to see such a document and none has been provided. Mr. Kingstad should not have been allowed to prevail with his motion on this involuntary bankruptcy.

I spoke with several attorneys and they all told me that my corporation did not need an attorney present to defend my corporation when fraud is being committed and the court must follow the "rule of law". Mr. Kingstad; has no judgment as he so claimed, under oath of perjury. How can the court even give this consideration without any evidence and participate in this scam? Instead of holding him accountable for his fraud and contempt of court, you reward him for his criminal conduct.

Nobody is above the law, Mr. Hedback. Not only was this a complete bogus claim, but not timely or properly filed. I received no timely notice and then Mr. Kingstad lies about the date of mailing. In my opinion this is just more politics disguised as a judicial process.

This is the same "day in court" that I had in Aymar's bankruptcy, (His third bankruptcy according to my investigator and Mr. Leonard was the trustee in all of them) Federal court case # 03-46682, Brian Leonard, trustee in that matter was complicit in allowing Mr. Aymar to commit perjury and fraud and steal my property and vacate a $600,000 judgment that I had against him. I am attaching reports from two investigators who found that Mr. Aymar had committed fraud, one investigator was a retired U.S. Marshal (Dennis Gauthier of GNA) He did the work for Mr. Leonard in the investigation and all Mr. Leonard had to do was "enforce the rule of law", but instead he rewards Mr. Aymar's fraud by giving him my property. The investigation shows that Mr. Aymar made millions by equity stripping my property with fraudulent mortgages, paid no state or federal taxes, lied under oath about his income (See attached reports of my investigators) I will be looking to Mr. Leonard personally for my losses which are in excess of one million dollars. This is justice, Mr. Hedback?

That's my day in court? There's more, a lot more, but I think that we have a pattern here in that most of the judges at both state and federal level are primarily Republican appointed judges and Mr. Kingstad, as attorney representing City Planners was party to most of the lawsuits. That in itself, should at least raise a pink flag. The courts here are equally complicit by suborning perjury by Mr. Kingstad in preventing blacks from taking up residency. He is nothing more than a government stooge performing like a circus monkey and the justice system applauds and rewards his performances of thievery.

Under this Administration it appears that, we have a Department of Corruption instead of a Department of Justice.

Under title U.S.C. Section 242-Deprivation of Rights under Color of Law, this Statute makes it a crime for any person acting under "Color of Law" statute, ordinance regulation or customs to willfully deprive or cause to be deprived from any person those rights privileges or immunities secured or protected by the Constitution and laws of the U.S.

Clearly, this has been a political process and I did not have my day in court as you so stated. I believe at this point my only day in court will be in the "court of public opinion".

I reject the notion that you can simply tie up my property illegally for well over a year. I want it released. Thank you in advance.

(signed by Marlene Fearing)

I also wrote letter to Judge O'Brien in this matter:

Dear Judge O'Brien:

As 100% owner of the corporate stock of Progressive Real Estate, Inc. I have not been able to use my land to complete the development because it has been tied up with this fraudulent claim initiated by Mr. Kingstad upon this court. I have repeatedly asked Mr. Hedback, the trustee in this matter to provide me with proof of the judgment that Mr. Kingstad alleges exists in the amount of $414,000. There is no record of such a judgment and Mr. Hedback has not provided me with such evidence.

I am requesting that my land be released and this case closed. It has been tied up for well over a year. Thank you in advance. Please find attached documents for the court record.

Respectfully submitted,
Marlene Fearing

NOTE: As of this writing, this case which involves my corporation is unresolved and it will soon be two years that my land has been tied up. I see this as yet another "land grab" by the government to take my last remaining assets. When we have the U.S. Department of Justice complicit in such thievery, it's a very sad day for America.

LAWSUIT # 8
Case # C2-05-6885
Eviction Action
Michael Aymar
Property Holding, LLC
v.
Marlene Fearing

In this action, Judge Doyscher ruled that my home should go to the bank even though I had not taken the mortgage and the land belonged to me. The mortgage was taken fraudulently (proof was submitted at trial) and in violation of our contract by the builder (Michael Aymar) whom the City chose to replace me. My contract with Mr. Aymar explicitly prohibited Mr. Aymar from placing any mortgages on my property. Note: Mr. Whiteis of the First Title Advantage Company was party to the contract, party to the illegal mortgage taken by Mr. Aymar and in court testifies that he had no awareness of the "no mortgage clause" even though he did the closing. Amazingly, Judge Doyscher bought this story and ruled against me.

In this lawsuit, I was illegally evicted from my home. This was the property that Michael Aymar also claimed on his Chapter 7 bankruptcy petition that he had deeded away and no longer had any interest in. Judge Doyscher knew this as well and still he gave my house to Mr. Aymar

Mr. Brian Leonard, bankruptcy trustee was informed about Mr. Aymar's bankruptcy fraud by my investigators GNA. Mr. Leonard promised he would take action, but he did not. Attorney Mark Kallenbach was supposedly working with the trustee to get my deeds for the remaining lots back. I don't know what Mr. Kallenbach negotiated with the trustee but I never did get my deeds to the property. I subsequently hired attorney James Doran to reclaim the property through a sheriff foreclosure on three lots. What we have here is essentially a U.S. Bankruptcy Trustee aiding and abetting bankruptcy fraud once again by Michael Aymar. The players involved in the Property Holding, LLC are the same people Michael Aymar's attorney, John Westrick, First Advantage Title, President Thomas Whiteis, Michael Aymar and his brothers David Aymar and Mark Aymar who were responsible for the fraud committed on the purchase of the property on the initial contract.

Letter written to U.S. Bankruptcy Trustee, Brian Leonard

June 10, 2006

Re: Michael P. Aymar
Bankruptcy File # 03-46682

Dear Mr. Leonard:

If you will recall, both my Attorney, James Doran and I contacted you regarding more evidence of fraud committed by Mr. Aymar in his bankruptcy petition. The latest being that he essentially took title to my house. Mr. Aymar stated on his bankruptcy petition that Lot 13, which was to be a house that he constructed for me, according to our agreement was in bank foreclosure. That was simply not the case as my investigator, Dennis Gauthier pointed out to you. Mr. Aymar subsequently filed an addendum, claiming that he had deeded the property away and that he had no interest. In November, 2005, he claims that he holds title as fee simple owner. The house remains in his name today at the Washington County Recorder's office. How can that be when I had a $600,000. judgment against him? Where was my protection not only as a judgment creditor, but as a homeowner?

In our last conversation you told both Mr. Doran and me that you would check on this matter and get back to us. That Mr. Leonard was over six months ago. I was evicted from my home because you allowed Mr. Aymar to commit a fraud. Please call James Doran and let us know when you will be getting my home back to me.

Sincerely;
Marlene Fearing

Summation of Investigation by GNA that became court evidence

In reviewing transitions that take place between the Aymar Brothers and their business it is apparent that these entities are in fact one company, using several names and a shell organization to avoid full disclosure of their true identity. Each of the brothers is fully aware of all operation of each

entity and act for the other in his absence. Marc and David were also fully aware of the Judgment against Michael from judgment creditors and have knowingly transferred funds and assets to avoid their exposure to seizure. Marc and David are also fully aware that Michael is currently claiming a Chapter 7 (No Asset Bankruptcy) here again. He is allowed to enjoy an extravagant lifestyle and enjoying an income exceeding $150,000. per year while creating the appearance that he has no personal funds or assets. This is apparent by David claiming that the 35 foot Carver boat slipped at Mulberry Point Harbor is his own, while he actually has his own boat that is slipped at the same harbor, each at a cost of about $6,000. per year, not including the cable television service both David and Michael have wired onto their respective boats. Photographic evidence and other documents have been obtained to support each statement asserted.

It should also be noted that this agency, Gauthier, Nechodom, Anderson Inc., was hired to collect upon a judgment rendered within Washington County against Michael and his companies; however at no time did any person or agency imply that the Aymar brothers or their companies have done any of the activities that have been uncovered by this agency. It can only be concluded that this has been the "normal operations" of this business when it was initially investigated by this agency. Clearly these brothers have acted in unison and conspired to allow Michael to transfer funds and assets undetected by both creditors and the United States Bankruptcy Courts.

*   *   *

LAWSUIT # 9
Case # 82-C1-05-005789
Mark Kallenback
v.Marlene Fearing, et al

I received no notice of any court hearing so therefore, I received no due process. I attended a pre-trial conference, but I thought after my testimony it was clear that Mr. Kallenbach had no case. I received no more court information regarding any scheduled trial. This was a typical ploy which was used not only at the State level but at the federal level as well. (I didn't get an invitation to the party) Was the judgment that Mr. Kallenbach received against me his payoff for doing nothing to defend me and aiding in feeding me to the lions in case # CO-03-3415? The contract between Mr. Kallenbach and me was that he would be compensated a percentage of what he collected on the $600,000. He collected nothing because of his incompetence, so that is what his fee should have been—zero. The contract also stated that he would be compensated if I had terminated his service.

Attorney James Doran was witness during a court proceedings before Judge Armstrong, whereby I had filed a second motion for a Rule 11 Hearing against Attorney Kingstad which Mr. Kallenbach failed to do. Clearly, Mr. Kallenbach did not want to inform the court that Mr. Kingstad had no standing to initiate a lawsuit against me. He repeatedly asked me if I was firing him. And I repeatedly told him "No, you allowed this to escalate to a situation that is now out of control so you fix it". I knew that if I fired him my contract with him would then become on an hourly basis. There is no record that I fired him. In fact, the evidence was to the contrary, whereby he submitted a withdrawal of his representation to the court. There was also many emails between Mr. Kallenbach and myself where I repeated that even though I was terribly disappointed in his representation, that I still wanted him to make an effort to provide some sort of defense for me.

* * *

LAWSUIT # 10
Case C4-04-2049
Jaguar credit

I was jailed once again because a bench warrant was issued for Constructive Civil Contempt. I received no notice of any court appearance. There was a bogus affidavit of service presented to the judge claiming that I had been served, when I did not.

Why I became a subject of this lawsuit is quite interesting. I see this as further proof that indeed their existed an effort to "get me"—"beat me down", "terrorize and humiliate me" and portray me as a litigious individual and not law abiding. **I was never a party to a contract between named defendant and Jaguar.** So why a bench warrant was issued against me after a complete bogus affidavit presented to the court stating that I had been properly served suggests unclean hands once again. I had never lived at the address shown on the affidavit as my residence. Yet somebody signed an affidavit of service which is then presented to the judge as being a valid notice of service.

In the summer of 2007, I was at the court house gathering information on one of my cases. The clerk on duty asked me if I was the Marlena Fearing that filed a suit against judges at Washington County. I answered that indeed I was that Marlena Fearing. Suddenly out of nowhere, a sheriff's Deputy approached me and told me that I was under arrest and handcuffed me. When I asked him what I was being arrested for, he said he didn't know, but I would soon find out. When I inquired if I had any rights, he answered, "No". When I was taken to the sheriff's office to be booked in, I overheard a conversation between the deputy and who I perceived to be someone in command. This happened on a Friday and it appeared that someone wanted me held in jail until the following Monday and the Sheriff's Department was not very happy about that. I heard him say, "This is absolutely bullshit, why is there a warrant for her arrest on a civil matter? I want her out of here today so get her before a judge."

What ensued depicts yet another 'typical set-up' and 'prearranged outcome' of any legal proceedings that involves Marlena Fearing at this Washington County Court. While I am handcuffed and awaiting to be presented to Judge Susan Miles, a Washington County Defender approached me and said she was going to defend me. I told her that I didn't think that I would qualify for a public defender, but she insisted she was going to defend me in any event. She was a very nice young lady and she indeed tried to help me by trying to explain to this judge that there is a mistake and I should not be party to this action. She did manage to get me released, but I view this as just another "Dog and Pony Show" in an attempt to instill fear and terrorize me by having me arrested. ***Again what we have here is the court process being used as a political process for retribution.***

ATTORNEYS COMPLICIT IN RETALIATION AGAINST ME

I feel that the incompetence and negligence of my attorneys (Mr. Lemmons and Mr. Kallenbach) contributed heavily to the unfavorable outcome of litigation that I was involved in. They sold me out rather than defend the action. This is how the system locks arms and unites as I have found. These attorneys chose to cooperate with a broken and corrupt system rather than challenge it or the opposing counsel who was committing fraud and perjury. They provided no defense, they did not challenge the vicious character assassinations against me, nor did they point out to the court that these were bogus lawsuits brought in bad faith with no evidence to support such action. Therefore perjury and fraud were being committed and they did nothing.

It's as if they were all complicit in acting out this outrageous attack on me and the judicial process. They knew that attorney Kingstad had no authority to initiate any lawsuit in behalf of the Association, yet they filed no motions or made any court record of this matter. If an attorney does not defend his client from such attacks, or at least attempt another venue or make court record of what is taking place, the illegal process only escalates. Both, Mr. Kallenbach and Mr. Lemmons knew that 68 pages of my documents were missing from the files, but neither of them questioned the court as to there whereabouts. They also knew that the allegations against me had no merit or evidence to substantiate them, yet they allowed the cases to move forward, while their attorney meters ran. They also knew that all court case files involving me had been removed, even those that had been archived. Neither Mr. Lemmons nor Mr. Kallenbach raised these issues with the court. Mr. Kallenbach knew that City's agent Robert Swenson threatened that "I would soon be seeing Jesus", yet he neglected to inform authorities or report to the court. It was said in his presence, yet he did nothing to enter this into evidence, that his client's life was being threatened again.

Attorney Mark Kallenbach

Mr. Kallenbach was hired by GNA (Gauthier, Nechodem and Anderson—investigators and collection agency) to collect on the $600,000. judgment against Michael Aymar and his many phony corporations; an award I received due to non appearance in court by Mr. Aymar. When the lawsuit was initiated against me by City Planners, Mary Parr and Robert Swenson illegally hiding behind the Homeowner's Association., Mr. Kallenbach agreed to defend me. Rather than defending me, he participated in the attack against me as evidence now reveals. This is what he knew and what he failed to do.

1. *Complicit in allowing a bogus lawsuit against me.* Mr. Kallenbach knew that the bogus lawsuit was illegal and was a complete fraud and the testimony given by the City Planners and their attorney Jon Erik Kingstad were offering perjured testimony. Mr. Kallenbach knew that Attorney Kingstad had no legal standing to represent the Homeowner's Association, yet he said nothing. Mr. Kallenbach knew that all allegations were false, yet he neglected to file a Rule 11 against Mr. Kingstad to point out the fraud being committed. He promised to file a motion with the court to expose the guilty parties, but he did not. This case went all the way to the U.S. Supreme Court with Mr. Kingstad representing the Homeowner's Association when he had been fired by the Association and told repeatedly that he had no standing to represent them.

2. *Failed to collect on Receivership.* Mr. Kallenbach acknowledged to Attorney James Doran that $60,000. had been located in a bank account registered to Michael Aymar. This money just disappeared and then Mr. Kallenbach had no explanation as to who took the money. Subsequently, Mr. Kallenbach filed to dismiss the receivership established to collect on my $600,000. judgment against Mr. Aymar. Who got the $60,000? Instead of Mr. Kallenbach collecting funds for me on the Receivership, I had to pay $5,000. to close the case. Something doesn't pass the smell test.

3. *Facilitated and enabled Aymar to get away with Bankruptcy Fraud.* Mr. Kallenbach knew that Aymar had illegally slandered title

to several pieces of my property, yet he did nothing to challenge his illegal bankruptcy. He filed nothing with the bankruptcy court to stop this thievery.

4. ***Kallenbach's own illegal slander of title with Attorney lien.*** Mr. Kallenbach was to be compensated by 20% of what he collected on the $600,000. judgment. He collected nothing, however, he slandered my title with an attorney lien. I received no notice of any court hearing so therefore, I received no due process. Was his judgment that he received against me from Judge Doyscher his reward for doing nothing to defend me and aid in feeding me to the lions in case # CO-03-3415? The contract between Mr. Kallenbach and me was that he would be compensated a percentage of what he collected on the $600,000. He collected nothing because of his incompetence, so that is what his fee should have been—zero. The contract also stated that he would be compensated if I had terminated his service.

Attorney Chad Lemmons

1. Chad Lemmons also knew that the bogus lawsuits were illegal and a complete fraud and the testimony given by the City Planners and their attorney Jon Erik Kingstad was therefore perjured testimony. He should have filed a Rule 11 to expose the guilty parties, but he did not.

2. Chad Lemmons failed to docket the $600,000 judgment against Aymar. He knew that Aymar and his accomplices were defrauding me and he failed to inform the courts. When I discovered that Mr. Aymar was taking out mortgages on my property, I personally filed an Adverse Claim on the remainder of the property. When Mr. Lemmons discovered that I filed such adverse claims, he became upset with me and insisted that I remove those claims. What this essentially did was to allow Mr. Aymar to move forward with more mortgages on those lots as well. Mr. Lemmons conduct in this matter enabled Mr. Aymar to further slander my property and facilitate his efforts to steal my equity.

3. Mr. Lemmons could have saved my home, but instead he aids in facilitating the foreclosure. All he had to due to save my home was to foreclose on my $600,000. judgment against Aymar since title to this

property was still in his name and he could have used the judgment to foreclose. This is so mind boggling as to why my own attorneys committed such transgressions against me. Who were they really working for and again the question becomes, why?

4. Mr. Lemmons also stipulated to a dismissal of a case involving one of Mr. Aymar's shell corporation, MRES when he knew that Mike Aymar was the President. I provided evidence to Mr. Lemmons that I gathered from the State Licensing Division which indicated that Mr. Michael Aymar was indeed the registered owner of MRES. Yet to the court Mr. Michael Aymar and his brother Mr. Marc Aymar switch identity of true owner to commit yet another fraud upon the court. This was so typical of their behavior, passing and switching ownership to conceal assets including to the U.S. Bankruptcy court. Mr. Lemmons never provided this evidence to the court and instead makes a deal to dismiss MRES.

5. Mr. Lemmons repeatedly failed to defend or protect me against bogus lawsuits by not presenting proper evidence to the court. He has a lot of explaining to do for this incompetence and negligence.

DEMOCRACY OR HYPOCRISY ?

It is not the American people that are destroying our nation with hatred and racial intolerance, it is our government at every level. We can put a man on the moon, but we cannot as a nation get discrimination under control? Something is wrong with that story. We certainly don't need more laws. We do not enforce the existing "rule of law" as was the situation in my case. America can accomplish anything that it sets its course on doing. We just haven't put our priorities in the correct place as yet. Defending Democracy, Freedom's cause, and speaking the truth in America should not be dangerous to your health; but in my case that was all too much a reality. There was no governmental agency, no law enforcement, and no court of law; not even a politician that I could go to and seek help because they were either complicit or unwilling to jeopardize their own political career by exposing the corruption. This madness was exacerbated by a big duck (John Jansen) in a little pond (Lake St. Croix Beach) and the corruption worked its way up the chain of command from there. Actually it worked both ways, from the top on down as well. It was evident to attorneys that I sought legal advice from, as they all stated to me after reviewing the evidence, that I had apparently stepped on some fairly 'big toes' to prompt this kind of reaction and retaliation. And they wanted no part of it for fear their legal practice and career would be jeopardized. *I was completely flabbergasted as to how I could step on anyone's toes when I was merely trying to uphold "Fair Housing Laws"?*

Just the mention of my name at any governmental agency at every level, set off a "red alert", signaling to all those involved to avoid me like the plague. It was cover-up after cover-up to hide what was really taking place behind closed doors even at the federal level. I never really meant to strike such fear in the hearts of our government officials for them to react with such indifference when I reminded them that we had a Constitution. If they had nothing to hide, why should they fear such a little "Nobody" like me? That is how they addressed me. Fearing is a "Nothing" and "Nobody", she owns nothing. Of course not, after they took everything away from me with their fraudulent and bogus lawsuits. I didn't have judges in my pocket like they did.

Agency/Departmental Malfeasance

Even after both MDHR, HUD and U.S Justice closed the discrimination files, I made many subsequent attempts to bring in the state and federal enforcement agencies to assist me in enforcing fair housing laws. Both the Minnesota Department of Human Rights and the Department of Urban Development are useless governmental agencies that are grossly irrelevant when it comes to enforcing housing discrimination as it pertains to violations by government. Enforcement all depends on who is in office. Apparently the conservative approach is to ignore human rights violations. These people have a lot to cover-up so they huddle together and protect one another. My experience tells me that these agencies are merely a "clearing house" to sanitize corruption when committed by government because the directors are politically appointed positions.

I am not implying that the employees of these agencies are not doing their jobs. I have met some very committed people that I feel investigated my complaints thoroughly and wanted to file charges against the City, but that required approval from their politically appointed directors. That's when the politics enter into the picture. (The Germans have a saying, "A crow will never pick out the eyes of another crow") I think that fairly sums up my experience with enforcement agencies, because they are politically appointed and they protect one another even when evidence of criminal wrong-doing is evident. Who is going to report this, the news media? Heck no, such action may cost them a sale of a newspaper or an irate sponsor canceling their TV advertisement. Bottom line, it's all about the money.

The City attorney certainly wasn't going to prosecute agents from the City who are violating state and federal laws; so he was part of the problem.

Washington County Attorney Douglas was made aware of the problem. I paid him numerous visits, wrote letters explaining to him what was taking place. Attorney James Doran also went with me to report the illegal conduct and transgressions against me. Mr. Douglas indicated that he would look into my allegations. His looking into it was essentially writing me a letter and telling me that if I insisted on Mary Parr and Robert Swenson being prosecuted, then he would have to consider prosecuting me for defending the black family and accusing me of acting as an attorney. In other words, I didn't even have the right to defend myself or the black family. That's justice in Lake St. Croix Beach and Washington County.

Excerpts from a letter written to Douglas Johnson, Washington County Attorney dated April 7, 2005

Dear Mr. Johnson:

This letter is a follow up to our phone conversation of yesterday, whereby, I requested answers to why I am not receiving equal protection under the law. Evidence will show that I am being attacked and retaliated against for upholding State and Federal housing laws, while those that are committing crimes of hate against me are being protected. You asked me to provide information with supporting documentation so you could investigate the matter. Before I outline the chain of events of illegal transgressions against me, I think it important that I provide you with some background information.

The attacks and threats to me of bodily harm and property damage started at the same time that I refused to evict the blacks. Sheriff reports will show that from June to November 2003, my property was repeatedly vandalized, windows broken, doors kicked in, a water fountain destroyed and my marketing signs defaced. After my continued efforts to repair them, Mary Parr had them destroyed totally by cutting them down with a chain saw on Thanksgiving Day, 2003. Witnesses to that were Larry Hall and his son. Sheriff reports will show that Mary Parr gave conflicting stories, claiming the City gave her approval and then the association gave her approval. The City, according to the sheriff reports, denies giving her such approval and there was never any board approval by the association. The City refused to prosecute and the County as well, claiming circumstantial evidence prohibited them from prosecuting. What evidence could possibly prevent a person from being prosecuted for a felony? The cost to replace those signs today is $8,575.00. This was

yet another attempt to prevent me from doing business. The City clerk admitted to the sheriff that there was no reason for those signs to be removed as I received permission from the City to erect those signs and the project is uncompleted with three remaining vacant lots.

Sheriff reports will also show that in July 2003 and 2004, Bob Swenson and Mary Parr took it upon themselves to hire a contractor and destroy wildflowers growing on my vacant lots, claiming they had authority by the City because they were deemed to be noxious weeds. How is it that on my property they are noxious weeds and in the watershed they are wildflowers, same seeding that I planted there as on the lots with City approval? When I attempted to stop Swenson from trespassing on my property he became so enraged, he jumped in his car which was parked in his driveway and sped in my direction, attempting to hit me and at the very last second, he swerved his car away. This was witnessed by Edith Ryan and Kaye Smith and reported to Sheriff Deputy Becky Engel. Both the City and the County refused to charge Swenson with aggravated assault. Mr. Swenson also assaulted (a friend of mine) and again to me on another occasion in 2004, as well as to my grandson Brandon Fearing. (Swenson was finally arraigned by an Oakdale Prosecutor and charged with assault on my grandson Brandon Fearing). The City and the County again refused to prosecute him because it was considered to be a conflict according to the Sheriff Deputy.

In the summer of 2004, both Mary Parr and Robert Swenson were observed by my neighbors, stalking and harassing me, i.e. parking outside my driveway and taking pictures, giving obscene gestures, blocking the driveway and yelling at potential clients "not to buy" as "wrong people" are moving in. The Sheriff had to be called once again to have them trespassed off the property. There were many such incidents and many did not even get reported because it became obvious to all those who observed this, that Parr and Swenson were "above the law" and nothing would be done to them anyhow. So why report?

I feel I should be entitled to the same protection under the law as any other U. S. Citizen, but clearly I am not. I believe as the above shows, I am not getting equal justice and equal protection, but rather those who are attacking me for upholding fair housing laws, are being protected. I am requesting that both Parr and Swenson are prosecuted for the following:

1. **Perjury**—Affidavits show among numerous other things, (1) that this project was never a 55 community, (2) that I never owed the Association money, but rather the association owed me, (3) that Parr and Swenson never had authority to initiate a lawsuit against me. They repeatedly committed a fraud upon the court by offering perjured testimony to the courts which resulted in court action (based on these lies) that would deny blacks housing.
2. **Harassment, Threats, Intimidation and Stalking**—After a court hearing in Washington County, Robert Swenson in the presence of my attorney Mr, Kallenbach threatened that "Fearing will be seeing Jesus if she calls and reports him to the sheriff again". Affidavits and police reports clearly show a consistent pattern by both Parr and Swenson of repeated attacks on me personally as well as to my property.
3. **Assault**—Sheriff Reports will also show that Swenson used his vehicle as a lethal weapon against my grandson and me as well as my friend.

I am attaching numerous affidavits as well as a witness list of those who have witnessed what has transpired. If you need further information of documentation please let me know.

Sincerely,
Marlene Fearing

*   *   *

Excerpts of letter written to Governor Pawlenty April 1, 2004

Office of Governor Tim Pawlenty
Re: MDHR—Housing Discrimination

Dear Governor Pawlenty:

Thank you for requesting that MDHR Commissioner Ms. Korbel reply to my letter of November 15, 2003. I have responded to her letter today of which I am forwarding a copy as well to you. While Ms. Korbel denies my allegations that both the Cities of Hastings and Lake St. Croix Beach violated Fair Housing laws, my rebuttal and attached affidavits tell quite a different story from people in the know (Mayors who witnessed the discrimination).

I am requesting that an investigation be conducted as to why my rights were not protected when I refused to participate with the two aforementioned Cities in their efforts to implement unfair and illegal housing practices. Ms. Korbel acknowledges the lengthy duration and she's correct. But the reason it is still on going is because no enforcing agency, for whatever reason, has made any effort to stop them. I personally have had to endure the wrath of retaliation by both Cities for telling them that their housing policies violate Federal and State Housing Laws. It's up to the MDHR to do that, not me.

Sincerely,
Marlene Fearing

Excerpt from letter written to Minnesota Assistant Attorney Generals Office

April 1, 2004

Mr. Richard Varco, Jr.
Assistant Attorney General
525 Park Street—Suite 200
St. Paul, MN 55103

Re: MDHR—Housing Discrimination

Dear Mr. Varco:

I spoke to you a couple of weeks ago regarding the unlawful housing violations that are still ongoing in the City of Lake St. Croix Beach and the retaliation directed at me for attempting to eradicate it. I also reiterated my same experience with the City of Hastings and the inability of the MDHR to take action to enforce Fair Housing Law in these Cities. You indicated that I should try again as now there is a new Commissioner and perhaps things will be different this time.

I have had communication from her now that the Governor has taken an interest in this matter. But as you can see from the tone of her letter the MDHR is in a state of denial. It's much easier to suggest that my allegations have no merit. Therefore, I am attaching my letter to her as well as affidavits from those who also support my position that Unfair Housing practices did and do exist and I am attacked for daring to challenge their illegal conduct. Since it doesn't look as though I will get any assistance from the MDHR, I am again asking the Attorney General's Office to intervene. The laws of this State are being violated and since there seems to be no local enforcement, I am looking to the State Attorney General for assistance.

Sincerely,
Marlene Fearing

*   *   *

Excerpt of letter written to Minnesota Attorney General Mike Hatch

Mr. Mike Hatch
Minnesota Attorney General
525 Park Street—Suite 200
St. Paul, MN 55103

Dear Mr. Hatch:

My name by now should be a familiar one to this Department given my numerous attempts to notify this office of the ongoing discrimination against minorities in this State by Government officials and retaliations against me for defending their right to fair housing. I've also had many conversations with Richard Varco, Jr. your Assistant Attorney General as I was refused a meeting with you to explain not only the gravity but the extent of the problem. When we have a judicial system that facilitates the discrimination and recrimination process by manipulation or destruction of evidence by judges, then I believe that calls for intervention by the State Attorney General's Office. Instead what we get is a strong defense of those actions. So bottom line what we have here is not only a tolerance, but an outright acquiescence of discrimination in this State by the highest agency of enforcement.

How is it that you can take on corruption in the corporate world but you can't expose corrupt judges who under the color of law have broken the law? The City of Lake St. Croix Beach is 100% Caucasian and Washington County, the judicial seat is 99.99% Caucasian. From what I have witnessed that has been made possible with the assistance of *some* racist Washington County Judges. This particular incident (many others) all started with a Republican appointed Judge, Mary Carlson appointed by her brother-in-law, Governor Arne Carlson, doing favor for another Republican comrade, John Jansen, former Washington County Judge who runs Lake St. Croix Beach. Judge Mary Carlson declared the project a senior project (MDHR and HUD declared the age restrictions unconstitutional) which allowed the City and the Association to evict the only blacks (under 55) in the community. Problem is that only the blacks under 55 were evicted and all the whites got "special waivers" to stay. Then she retires, and other judges trying to cover and protect her illegal actions, get caught up in aiding and abetting the corruption. When I protested the illegal eviction of blacks, I am given 30 days in jail. When they don't like the message, they try to demonize the messenger. Further recrimination against me for my whistle blowing is then judges have suborned perjury and retaliated by taking away my property holdings with bogus judgment awards against me, when evidence is clear that the original complaints were a complete fraud upon the court. So essentially what has happened is that the attorney representing the City's agents is awarded for fraud and perjury. Additionally, this same attorney is now defending the Washington County court appointed mediator in federal court that was responsible for violating my Constitutional rights in denying me a right to vote as a homeowner. Entire case files of mine, even those that were archived have magically disappeared for obvious editing. Problem they have with that is there are too many witnesses to what transpired in the courtroom. How can this be happening in Minnesota?

In my conversations with Mr. Varco, he has repeatedly explained that the Attorney General's Office can not take enforcement action against discrimination unless probable cause is found by the Minnesota Department of Human Rights (MDHR). The problem with that is twofold, the MDHR Director is not only politically appointed, but the ineptness of the Department is a story in itself. It's not that they don't have dedicated and conscientious people working for them and trying to do the right thing, like Elaine Hansen and Eric Falk who found "Probable

Cause" only to find that Politics trumped those findings and all their efforts were in vain. *This shouldn't be about Democrats or Republicans; it should be about enforcing the laws.* If you don't know the extent of the problem, I suggest you review federal court files of which I am attaching the complaints filed in federal court. By the way, in case # 06-CV-456 JNE/JJG an attorney from your office, John Garry has recently made a motion to dismiss my lawsuit against the district court, which not only violated State and Federal Housing Laws, but U.S. Constitutional laws as well. *I am asking you to withdraw that motion and instead take action against the perpetrators.*

I can fully appreciate and understand that it is the duty of the Attorney General's Office to defend a State entity, but I think that should only apply if they have violated no laws. By the same token, you have taken an oath to uphold the laws and defend and protect the rights of all people in Minnesota which includes minorities, did you not? We have violations of both state and federal law by those who are supposed to uphold the law. And they get a free pass to do it all over again simply because they are part of a corrupt system? So in other words, a judge who has broken the law gets preferential treatment as opposed to Minnesota Citizens who have been wronged by the corruption? I suspect that this is a trend rather than one isolated incident in this State and has more than likely been taking place long before your tenure. It has grown to this "monster" today because we have not had an Attorney General willing to take action and set an example that this kind of outrageous judicial manipulation will not be tolerated. Judges are not above the law, or are they in Minnesota?

I am also attaching letters written by Attorney James Doran, who once worked as an attorney for the Attorney General Office, to HUD investigators who found housing violations and forwarded the complaint up to the U.S. Justice Department for prosecution. I think you will find his letters helpful in terms of the extent of the problem. Their position is, however, that this is a Minnesota problem that needs to be fixed by Minnesota. *The buck has been passed so many times, there is no ink left.*

The thought has occurred to me that the corruption could reach levels higher than I wish or care to think possible, and those who have been harmed may never see justice. That is why I am writing of my experience as events unfold through affidavits, letters, taped conversations and court documents. The truth will be made known. Since the "Free Press" is apparently not so free, my plan is to initiate my own internet news blogging and promote my book as well. The final judge in this matter may well be the people of Minnesota, after reading and hearing about my experience and they can decide who stays in office and who would do better in Mississippi.

Since my life (and my family's) have been threatened by agents for the City and I get no police protection from Washington County or this State, I am living in exile. Therefore, the only means of communication with me is by email: May I hear from you soon?

Sincerely.
Marlene Fearing

I never received a response from The Attorney general's Office, instead they continued in its defense of the Washington County Judges that were named in the lawsuit that the Black family and I initiated in federal court.

THE COURTS WERE USED POLITICALLY FOR RETRIBUTION AGAINST ME FOR EXPOSING GOVERNMENT CORRUPTION

The numerous bogus lawsuits that were initiated against me as described in the litigation section of this documentary, to take my land and my assets could not have been accomplished without the aid of the Judges at Washington County district court.

If it wasn't bad enough that such a corrupt judicial process existed at a local State level, but it seems this madness exists at the federal level as well. I appealed every case as far as I could take it—from local state district courts to state appellate court and on up to the federal level. Interesting that all my cases at the federal level were assigned to Republican judges as well, particularly those appointed by President Bush and his Republican Congress.

As a licensed general contractor, developer and builder I am mandated to uphold fair housing laws, yet that is exactly why I was jailed. What was my crime? As President of a Homeowner's Association, I wrote a letter to all homeowner's protesting the eviction of blacks. It's amazing how a corrupt judge with just a stroke of a pen can render such an unlawful and unjust opinion by ignoring the laws and changing the evidence in her findings to achieve the desired result—evict blacks illegally. She found me guilty of meddling with "Association affairs" when in reality I wrote a letter protesting the eviction of a black family. In my opinion, she made her racist views be known with her judicial spin. **What we have essentially is a corrupt enterprise disguised as judges. And we call them "Honorable"? What's honorable about violating State and Federal Law and politicizing the judicial process?**

The eviction was clearly racially motivated by a racist City and its planners and I stated as much in my letter. To evict an owner under the pretext of some bogus violation was the quintessential act of racial discrimination and despicable human behavior that I have witnessed in quite some time. Yet that is exactly what happened with the blessing of all those agencies (both state and federal) to oversee such illegal activities as well as the judicial process. This is not how the process should work. Rather than holding those responsible and accountable for their actions (government entities) the evidence is twisted and distorted to achieve the desired result or the evidence itself takes on a missing status and disappears entirely. I also found it interesting how so many witnesses to the fact, suddenly became stricken with selective amnesia, including two of my attorneys.

When the U.S. Justice Department under the Bush Administration closed the File on gender and racial discrimination, I brought suit against the City of Lake St. Croix in federal court. I sued for gender discrimination and the taking of my land by the City of Lake St. Croix Beach for a public watershed without compensation. According to attorneys that I sought for representation indicated that my case should be a slam dunk since the Supreme Court already ruled that a City can't take land from a developer without compensation.

The taking of my land for public use without just compensation is prohibited by a Supreme Court decision on June 24, 1994, whereby Chief Justice William Rehnquist, speaking for a 5-4 majority stated that, "forcing developers to give up their land violates the Fifth Amendment that private property (shall not) be taken for public use without just compensation".

The judge appointed to hear the case was Judge Joan Ericksen, appointed by President Bush in 2002. Even though we asked for a trial by jury, we were denied that and instead this judge ruled from the bench with a Summary Judgment in favor of the City. According to the PFAW report, "Confirmed Judges—Confirmed Fears" judges appointed by President Bush who have established a record of violating judicial due process laws; this is a typical and predictable outcome from his appointed judges, to cover up any wrongdoing with rulings of "Summary Judgments, "res judicata" or complete dismissals without foundation for such action.

I appealed to the 8th circuit court File # 06-2300. The panel assigned to hear the case consisted of two more judges appointed by Bush and his Republican

Congress that also made the report as judges who violated due process laws. They affirmed Judge Joan Ericksen's Decision.

The black family and I decided that we were not going to sit back and allow such civil liberties abuses and have our properties to be taken from us without a fight. By that time they had lost their home due to a racist City and Judge Mary Carlson when they were evicted because their children were black. I also had lost my home with the help of the City's chosen developer, Michael Aymar, Bankruptcy Trusee, Brian Leonard and Judge Doyscher.

Since the U.S. Justice Department refused to protect our rights under the Constitution, the Black family joined me in a federal lawsuit in Federal District Court in Minneapolis. (My reference to these folks as the "Black Family" or Mary and John Doe is because of their minor children, I wish to not identify the name for fear of further retribution to the children involved)

Case # 06-CV-456 JNE/JJG

The judge assigned to this case was none other than Judge Joan Ericksen. Of all the judges that would have ruled according to the "Rule of Law" and the evidence, we are given another Bush appointee.

The Complaint is as follows:

Marlene Fearing, Progressive Real Estate,	**Case Type: 42 U.S.C. Sec. 1983 &**
Mary and John Doe	**Others**

CASE # 06-CV-456 JNE/JJG.,

Plaintiffs,

JURY DEMAND

v.

Lake St. Croix Villas Homeowner's Associaton, Mary Parr, Robert Swenson, Arlene Swenson, et al. **COMPLAINT**

Defendants.

TO: THE COURT AND DEFENDANTS.

For their Complaint, Plaintiffs Marlene Fearing, Mary and John Doe Allege the following:

COUNT I

On or about September 10, 2003, Plaintiffs Mary and John Doe received a complaint from Defendant Mary Parr, President of Defendant Lake St. Croix Villas Homeowner's Association and City Planner for Defendant City of Lake St. Croix Beach, stating that they were in violation of the age restrictions, and anti-children clause of the Development Contract and the Homeowner's Association which supposedly had a 55 years or older age restriction and restricted the number of occupants.

Plaintiff Does were required to attend a Homeowner's Association Hearing at the nearby Methodist Church on September 24, 2003. Plaintiff Does were not allowed to address the Board at the Hearing. Defendants Mary Parr or Arlene Swenson would repeatedly yell "Shut Up, this is a Hearing, not a Meeting and you cannot speak". And anyone friendly to the Does situation were also repeatedly threatened with arrest by the Board Members, Mary Parr and Arlene Swenson. Plaintiff Does were owners and even though there were many renters occupying many of the twin homes who also had children and were under the age of 55, they received no such Hearing (Including President, Tony Thooft who had two minor children living with him) for their violations from Defendants Parr, Swenson who had control of the Homeowner's Association. Shortly after the meeting, Plaintiff Does received a letter from Mary Parr that stated that due to their violation of the rules they would be subject to fines of $10.00 a day for being under age and $10.00 a day for having children.

At the time they purchased their twin home, John Doe was 53 years of age And Mary Doe was 50 years of age. They had four children living with them on a permanent basis, all of whom were African-American.

As a result of the letter sent by Defendant Homeowner's Association and Defendant Parr, Plaintiff Does were forced to leave their home because they could not afford such Draconian assessments.

Upon information and belief the Does have learned that after they were forced to leave, other homeowners under the age of 55 years of age have been granted a waiver by the Homeowner's Association and continue to reside therein even if they are not in compliance. The homeowner's under 55 (Caucasian) who were granted a waiver are;

1. Tony Thooft—(mid forties)
2. Brian Willaims—(mid forties)
3. Terry Williams—(forties)
4. Marco Ironi—(forties)
5. Aaron Schwinn—(forties)
6. Heather Schwinn—(forties)
7. Bobbie Carey—(forties)

Upon information and belief, none of these people were asked to attend a Hearing or were threatened with expulsion or fines. The only difference between their situation and Plaintiff Does were that they were white with *NO* black children and the Does were white with black children.

Defendant Homeowner Association claims that the Does were in violation of the Fair Housing Act, 42 United States Code Section 3601, et seq. for violating the 55 year or older requirements. Plaintiff Does maintain that the Defendant Homeowner's Association, Mary Parr, Robert Swenson, acting as City Planners for Defendant City of Lake St. Croix Beach did "under color of law" deprive Plaintiff Does of their First Amendment right to speak, their right of property ownership under the Fifth Amendment and their right of equal protection and due process under the Fifth, Fourteenth Amendment of the Constitution, all in violation of Section 1983 of Title 42 U.S.C Code and Civil Rights Act of 1968, U.S. Code Section 3613.

COUNT II

That Plaintiff Progressive is the fee owner of lots 1, 2, and 3 Block 1, St. Croix Villas and Marlene Fearing also claims an interest in Lot 13, Block 1, St. Croix Villas. That Plaintiffs Marlene Fearing and Progressive were at one time the Declarant of the Townhouse Association until May 4, 2001.

That Plaintiff Does asked Marlene Fearing for help when the Defendants Homeowner's Association and Mary Parr attempted to evict the Does for alleged violation of the Declaration and Bylaws.

That as a result of Marlene Fearing attempting to defend the Does and their right to stay in their home, Defendants Mary Parr, Robert Swenson, Arlene Swenson purportedly acting under the Authority of The Homeowner's Association on May 8, 2003 brought a lawsuit to evict Defendants Fearing and Progressive from their lands alleging violation of Minn. Stat. 515B and 42 US Code Section 3601 et. Seq.

Plaintiff Fearing who is white has an African-American Grandson who often stays with her.

Plaintiff Fearing verily believes that the lawsuit against her by Defendant Parr, Swensons, and the Homeowner's Association was a ruse in retaliation of her defense of the Plaintiff Does rights to live in peace in their own home.

That at the time that Defendants Parr, Swenson initiated the lawsuit against Plaintiff Fearing and Progressive, they were not members in good standing, they were not on the Board as Directors and Defendant Jon Erik Kingstad had full knowledge that his clients had no authority to sue on behalf of the Homeowner's Association, yet they offered perjured testimony and essentially committed a fraud upon the State District Court. At the time that the lawsuit was initiated against Fearing and Progressive, the Board consisted of Marlene Fearing, President, Edith Ryan, Vice president and Ted Perlinger, Secretary-Treasurer. They had absolutely no standing as Representatives of the Association nor even members as both were delinquent in their assessments.

That Defendants Jon Erik Kingstad as attorney for Parr, Swenson acting as City Planners for Defendant City of Lake St. Croix Beach an entity that had many disputes with Plaintiff Fearing over development issues, discriminatory violations (Fed. Court File CV04-5127) also saw this as an opportunity to get rid of Ms. Fearing.(Ex. 2) an affidavit from Theodor Perlinger who overheard one of John Jansen's many threats (a retired Judge of Washington County) former County Attorney, Mayor of Lake St. Croix Beach) directed at Defendant Fearing that she would never prevail in Washington County because he knows every judge personally.

Defendants, Attorney Jon Erik Kingstad, Parr, Swenson, the Homeowner's Association and the City of Lake St. Croix Beach acting under the color of 42 U.S.C Section 3601 attempted to deprive Plaintiffs

Fearing and Progressive of their rights in violation of their Constitutional Rights under the Fifth and Fourteenth Amendment of the U.S. Constitution, 42 U.S.C. Chapter 21, Subchapter I Section 1983.

COUNT III

Plaintiffs allege that Defendants Parr, Swensons and their attorney, Jon Erik Kingstad acting on behalf of the Homeowner's Association and the City of Lake St. Croix Beach conspired to prevent Marlene Fearing from exercising her First Amendment Right. They arranged to obtain on or about November 24, 2003 a court order from the District Court of Washington County prohibiting Plaintiff Marlene Fearing from intervening on behalf of the Does impending eviction.

On or about June 15, 2004, Marlene Fearing sent a letter addressed to all "Neighbors" defending the right of Plaintiff Does to live in their home from which they were facing eviction.

Defendant Washington County District Court issued an Order stating that Marlene Fearing's letter to the Homeowner's violated the initial court order and Judge Mary E. Hannon ordered Defendant Fearing to 30 days in Jail, which was stayed if she paid a $500.00 fine.

Plaintiff Fearing refused to pay the fine since the order was in violation of her First Amendment right of free speech and accordingly was ordered to jail by Defendant Washington County District Court, Judge Thomas Armstrong. Defendant Fearing's medication for a heart ailment was withheld from her during her incarceration.

Plaintiff Fearing seeks damages for violation of her right to free speech under the First Amendment and under 42 U.S. Code Section 1983, by conduct of the Washington County District Court, Defendants Parr, Swensons, their attorney Jon Erik Kingstad and the St. Croix Villas Homeowner's Association.

COUNT IV

On or about July, 2003, Defendant Washington County District Court appointed retired Judge Kenneth Maas to supervise Defendant Homeowner's Association election. There was no court order for subsequent court supervision of the Homeowner's Association elections in 2004 and 2005, yet Fearing was forewarned by Defendant Tony Thooft, President of Defendant Homeowner's Association if she attempted to attend, that she would be arrested and jailed. At the time of the meeting Defendant Thooft was the only officer representing the Association as the rest of the Board resigned. There was no quorum and no legal Association. Recent depositions in the District Court Case, reveal that Defendants Parr and Swenson had ex parte communications with Judge Maas and he attended and participated in supervising the elections of an illegal Board that denied Fearing a right to vote as a homeowner.

Defendant David Magnuson, acting on behalf of Defendant Washington County District prevented Marlene Fearing and Progressive from voting as members of the Association even though it was undisputed that Progressive was the fee owner of three lots and Fearing had ownership interest in lot 13, Block 1. Fearing was asked to leave the meeting or she would be arrested. Others who attempted to defend Ms. Fearing were threatened with arrest as well.

Accordingly in denying Plaintiff Fearing from voting, Defendant District Court (judges) and Defendant Tony Thooft as President of Defendant Homeowner's Association violated Plaintiff Fearing and Progressive Real Estate's right of property under the Fifth Amendment of the U.S. Constitution and 42 United States Code Section 1983 were violated under the "Color of Fair Housing Act".

COUNT V

On or about April 30, 2004, Judge Mary Carlson issued an order adjudicating the Homeowner's Association as a 55 and older project. In her findings the ages of many of the Homeowner's were reported as older than what was stated on the Affidavits of the owners. Despite the Judge's order, the Defendants Homeowner's Association, Parr, Swenson and their Attorney Jon Erik Kingstad have conspired to permit occupants under 55 who are all Caucasian to reside in the twin home project. This action is in clear violation of 42 U.S.Code Sections 3601 et seq. and in breach of their fiduciary duties under the Development Agreement, The Articles of Incorporation and Bylaws of Lake St. Croix Villas Homeowner's Association. Plaintiff Fearing seeks damages of equitable disgorgement of profits arising from the approval of sale of the improved and unimproved lots to persons under the age of 55 in violation of Defendant's Homeowners Association, Parr, Swenson and their attorney Jon Erik Kingstad's fiduciary duties, express and implied warranties and the limitations of the Minnesota Common Interest Ownership Act,

Minn. Stat. Section 515B.1-101-515B. 4-118, the development agreement and Declaration of Covenants and restrictions and conditions of Lake St. Croix Villas Homeowner's Association and the Minnesota nonprofit corporation Act. Minn. Stat. Sectrion 317A.001-317A 909.

COUNT VI

Plaintiff Fearing further alleges as follows:

That on or about November 29th, 2003 Defendant Mary Parr acting as agent of Defendant City of Lake St. Croix Beach and President of Homeowner's Association did cause to have destroyed marketing signs owned by Plaintiff's Fearing and Progressive. Plaintiff Fearing has suffered financially due to her inability to market her development. That the value of said sign which was located near the twin home project was in excess of $8500. which constitutes a felony. Defendant City of Lake St. Croix Beach refused to charge and prosecute Defendant Parr with the crime.

COUNT VII

That Plaintiff Fearing further alleges as follows:

That on July 7, 2003, and again on approximately January 20, 2005, Defendant Robert Swenson attempted to hit Plaintiff Fearing with his car and again while she was walking one evening, Plaintiff Swenson approached Fearing from behind with no lights on, causing Fearing to jump onto the curb for safety. Fearing feared for her life as Defendant's vehicle was used as a weapon in assaulting Fearing. Defendant City of

Lake St. Croix Beach also did not charge Defendant Robert Swenson with his crime of assault with intent to do bodily harm to Fearing.

*   *   *

Judge Joan Ericksen, refused to see or hear any evidence against any government official because to do so would violate their 11th amendment rights. No mention was made however, as to the violation of rights that the African-American family and I suffered by such "arrogant abuse of power." The tactic used by this judge had a familiar ring, same tactics as in Washington District Court—divide and conquer; and ignore the evidence. I was completely dismissed from the suit and the remainder of the suit was only against the Homeowner's Association in behalf of the Does. By this time, we already knew that this Judge was ruling on her own personal agenda and not by the "Rule of Law" or Constitutional Law.

We appealed to the 8th circuit court case # 06-4078. The appeal was denied. We asked for a rehearing. That was also denied because Judge Ericksen refused to give a final ruling. I was kept dangling until the Does issues were resolved. The three panel Judges assigned to hear this case at the 8th Circuit court were all judges that were appointed by George W. Bush.

The remainder of the case was still before Judge Joan Ericksen. Mary and John Doe asked the case to be dismissed because they knew that they would not get justice from this Judge. In fact they filed a Judicial Complaint against this judge with the U.S. District Court in Minneapolis as well as at the Eight Circuit court in Kansas City, Mo. The 8th circuit court rejected the complaint—the panel once again were all judges appointed by Bush.

When Judge Ericksen issued her order to close the case, I did not get notice from the court either by electronic filing or mailing, therefore we could not timely file for an appeal. This was not the first time this happened. Evidence will show that the Does and I have informed the court on numerous occasions of such actions. I requested an extension to file an appeal and Judge Ericksen denied it. I appealed that decision to the appellate court. They denied it as well. Again, all judges hearing this case were appointed by President Bush and his Repulican Congress and all made the list on PFAW report as judges in violation of due process laws.

NO. 08-1625

UNITED STATES COURT OF APPEALS
FOR THE EIGHTH CIRCUIT
MARLENE FEARING
MARY AND JOHN DOE
Plaintiff-Appellant

v.

LAKE ST. CROIX VILLAS HOMEOWNER'S
ASSOC., CITY OF LAKE ST. CROIX BEACH,
MARY PARR, ROBERT SWENSON,
WASHINGTON COUNTY DISTRICT COURT, et al
Defendants-Appellees

ON APPEAL FROM THE UNITED STATES DISTRICT COURT
DISTRICT OF MINNESOTA—HONORABLE JOAN ERICKSEN
CASE #06-CV-456

PETITION FOR REHEARING
MARLENE FEARING, APPEARING PRO SE

Plaintiffs Counsel
Marlene Fearing, Appearing Pro Se

Defendants Counsel

Jon Erik Kingstad, Esq.	**Jon K. Iverson, Esq.**	**John S. Garry, Esq.**
Suite 260	**9321 Ensign Ave. S.**	**Office, Attor. Gen.**
600 Inwood Ave. No.	**Bloomington, MN**	**445 Minn. Street**
Oakdale, MN 55128	**55438**	**St. Paul, MN 55101**

*   *   *

UNITED STATES COURT OF APPEALS

FOR THE 8TH CIRCUIT

Marlene Fearing
Progressive Real Estate, Inc.
Mary Doe and John Doe

Plaintiffs—Appellants

v.

Lake St. Croix Villas Homeowner's Assoc.
City of Lake St. Croix Beach,
Mary Parr, Robert Swenson,
Washington County District Court, et al

Defendants—Appellees

JURISDICTIONAL STATEMENT

This court takes jurisdiction of this case based upon the federal fair housing act in the 42 U.S.C. section 3601 et seq. and 42 U.S.C, Chapter 21, Subchapter 1, Section 1983 claims; and subject matter jurisdiction pursuant to 28 U.S.C. 1331 (2000) and 1332 (2000) (amended 2005). This case was initiated based upon civil rights violations against Appellant Does and continued retaliation and assaults on Appellant Fearing for her role in defending fair housing as outlined in Case No. 06-2300 and Case No.06-4078 both decided by the *same* judge, as this case, Judge Joan Ericksen. The civil rights violations claimed under 42 U.S.C. Sec. 1983 have a long history dating back years and the conduct of all defendants is so complicit and intertwined that it is difficult to determine where the conduct of one ends and the other begins. The list of the Defendants shows an ongoing pattern of a local governmental system locking arms in furthering their attacks on the Appellants, a violation of Title U.S.C., Section 242.

STATEMENT OF ISSUES

This appeal presents the following issues for review:

At issue is the conduct of Judge Joan Ericksen in preventing Appellants from use of the federal court—untimely notices or none at all and then a refusal to allow sufficient time for the appellants to submit a timely appeal.

1. Did Judge Ericksen's biases and prejudices prevent her from acting as a Judge, thereby denying Appellants due process guaranteed under the 5th and 14th Amendments?
2. Did she violate the "Rule of Law" when she acted on her own personal agenda, thus abandoning her duties in administering fair and equal treatment to all parties?
3. Did she violate the Plaintiffs right to a jury trial (guaranteed by the 7th Amendment) when she ruled with res judacata, complete dismissals and summary judgment and not allowing Plaintiffs to present any evidence?
4. Can a federal judge deny a U.S. Citizen access to a federal court as Judge Ericksen admitted herself in her orders?

5. Did Judge Joan Ericksen ignore the "Rule of Law" in granting immunity to government officials who violated both state and federal laws by dismissing claims against them (claiming 11th amendment protection) thereby rendering them, "Above the Law"?

6. Were Appellants denied due process by presiding Judge Joan Ericksen due to her obvious bias and prejudices as depicted in complaint filed against her at the 8th circuit court, Chief Judge James B. Loken? **Judge Ericksen acknowledged in her order of December 19, 2007, "The Court granted in part the defendants' motion and restricted Fearing's ability to commence litigation in this court". Was Fearing's Constitutional Right to due process under the 5th and 14th Amendment violated?**

PETITION FOR REHEARING BY PANEL (En Banc)

Appellant Fearing respectfully requests a new panel of judges for this Hearing.

Pursuant to Federal Rule of Appellate Procedure No. 40, Appellant Fearing hereby requests a rehearing in the dismissal of the appeal. The reason given by the 3—Panel Judges consisting of Judge Melloy, Judge Smith and Judge Benton was that the appeal is dismissed because it was untimely. If in fact the appeal is considered untimely, it is because Appellant Fearing received no notice from the court, either by mail or by electronic filing of the final order. This was not the first time that Appellants were denied mailings from the court. There appears to be a systemic problem in the court of Judge Joan Ericksen, unintentional or otherwise pertaining to timely notices to the Appellants. Appellant Does and Fearing have written to the court previously and complained of this problem. Appellant Fearing believes this was a deliberate ploy to sabotage efforts by the Appellants to seek justice in the court of law.

Pursuant to FRAP (4) 5(a) allows an Appellant to file for an extension of time. Appellant did file within the 30 days allowed for an extension of time due to health issues (Fearing) and Judge Ericksen denied such request. By her own admission, Judge Ericksen acknowledged in more than one order that, "she was restricting Fearing's ability to commence litigation in this court". That sentiment was the guiding force that

prohibited her from acting as a judge, but rather out of her own personal and political convictions, thereby ignoring the "Rule of Law".

Appellant Fearing was completely dismissed from this case in November 8, 2006, without having an opportunity to present any evidence. Appellant Fearing and the Does filed for an appeal Court No. 06-4078 and also a subsequent Petition for Rehearing, both were denied by Judges Wollman, Smith and Benton. Since Fearing had been completely dismissed, she should have been allowed to prevail on her appeal at that time since Judge Ericksen had already decided that Appellant Fearing would be denied her constitutional right to due process guaranteed under the 7th Amendment to the Constitution. Appellant Fearing considers this to be a clear act of judicial misconduct and just another act of aggression against Appellant Fearing to deny her access to the court process. This entire process does not pass the smell test and reeks of a political cover-up because many defendants in this case include judges and other elected officials who have violated State and Federal Laws regarding civil rights issues, fair housing laws, fraud and perjury.

Judge Ericksen's conduct was similarly displayed in another case that was assigned to her, Case # 04-CV-05127/ Appeals Court # 06-2300. Again this case was dismissed by 3-Panel judges Wollman, Colloton and Benton. Even though Fearing had the law and evidence on her side, Judge Ericksen was complicit in furthering Defendant City of Lake St. Croix Beach's efforts to steal some $900,000. from Fearing. Judge Ericksen didn't want to see the evidence in that case as well and ruled a Summary Judgment, without seeing any evidence. Fearing received no compensation from the City for the taking of her land which was prohibited by a Supreme Court Ruling on June 24, 1994, whereby Chief Justice William Rehnquist, speaking for a 5-4 majority, stated that forcing developers to give up their land violates the Fifth Amendment guarantee that private property (shall not) be taken for public use without just compensation. Essentially what we have here is a lower court trumping a Supreme Court Ruling. This shows not only the arrogance of this judge, but the fact that she is legislating from the bench which is not her right to do, but rather that of Congress.

This lawsuit was initiated by Plaintiffs Doe and Fearing as outlined in the original complaint. Evidence will show that Plaintiffs have repeatedly protested the bias by Judge Joan Ericksen in denying us our Constitutional Right to due process guaranteed by the 5th and 14th Amendments. The Plaintiffs were denied an opportunity to present our evidence to a Jury (a violation of our 7th Amendment rights) regarding the abuses by all Defendants named in this matter, including attorney

Jon Eric Kingstad, a City and Washington County District Judges who engaged in criminal conduct as outlined in the complaint.

On November 8, 2006, Judge Ericksen dismissed all claims except the Does' claims against The Association, Parr and Swenson under the Fair Housing Act. A clear act of "Divide and Conquer". How is it possible for Judge Ericksen to have ruled as she did when Plaintiffs in this matter were *not given an opportunity to present any evidence?* This was a protective cover-up by this Judge and she certainly did not want to see incriminating evidence against defendants many are people (connected to the government) who are engaged in criminal behavior. *Nobody is above the law.* Additionally she has repeatedly suborned perjury of legal counsel Jon Erik Kingstad as depicted in Case # 04-CV-05127, same judge, same attorney, Jon Erik Kingstad, same Defendant City of Lake St. Croix;

ARGUMENT

The truth lies in the evidence and testimony which Plaintiffs-Appellants were prevented from presenting to the court when the case was dismissed by Summary Judgment. Subsequently Plaintiff-Appellants were denied the right to file timely appeals when final orders were not submitted by the court. Plaintiffs were denied a right to a jury trial in violation of the 7th Amendment and denied due process in violation of their 5th and 14th Amendment Rights.

Here the record abounds with genuine issues of material fact that the court doesn't seem to want to see or hear. There were no pleadings, depositions or admissions in this case. It never got that far. This begs the question as to how was it possible for Judge Joan Ericksen to render the Finding and Orders without any review of the evidence? Clearly, her findings were based on her own prejudices, politics and not the "Rule of Law", thus making her rulings "void". There can be no "Rule of Law" when judicial accountability is absent. *Title 18 U.S.C. Section 242—Deprivation of Rights Under Color of Law.* This statute makes it a crime for any person acting under color of law, Statute, ordinance, regulation, or customs to willfully deprive or cause to be deprived from any person those rights, privileges, or immunities secured or protected by the Constitution and laws of the U.S. Acts under "color of any law" include acts not only done by federal, state, or local officials with the bounds or limits of their lawful authority, but acts done without and beyond the bounds of their lawful authority. (relevant portion) this definition includes, in addition to law enforcement officials, *individuals such as Mayors, Council persons, Judges, etc.*

Under Rule 12 (b)(6) of the Federal Rules of Civil Procedure, a court must accept the complaint's factual allegations as true and construe them in the light most favorable to the plaintiff. *Midwestern Mach., inc. v. Nw Airlines, Inc. 167F.3d 439, 441 (9th Cir. 1999): Davis v. Hall, 992 F.2d 151, 152 (8th Cir. 1993).* The court will not dismiss the complaint unless it appears beyond doubt that the plaintiff cannot prove any set of facts in support of his claim that would entitle him to relief. *Conley v. Gibson, 355 U.S. 41, 45-46 (1957); Schaller Tel. Co. v. Golden Sky Sys., Inc., 298 F.3d 736, 740 (8th Cir. 2002). Here the court was not amenable to hear or see any evidence that would support Plaintiff-Appellants position.*

Chandler v. Judicial Council of the 10th Circuit, 398 U. S. 74, 90 S. Ct. 1648, 26 L. Ed. 2d 100. Justice Douglas, in his dissenting opinion at page 140 said, "If (federal judges) break the law, they can be prosecuted." Justice Black, in his dissenting opinion at page 141) said, "Judges, like other people, can be tried, convicted and punished for crimes . . . *The judicial power shall extend to all cases, in law and equity, arising under this Constitution*".

Cooper v. Aaron, 358 U.S. 1, 78 S. Ct. 1401 (1958)

Note: Any judge who does not comply with his oath to the Constitution of the United States wars against that Constitution and engages in acts in violation of the supreme law of the land. The judge is engaged in acts of treason.

The U.S. Supreme Court has stated that "no state legislator or executive or judicial officer can war against the Constitution without violating his undertaking to support it". See also *In Re Sawyer,* 124 U.S. 200 (188); *U.S. v. Will,* 449 U.S. 200, 216, 101 S. Ct. 471, 66 L. Ed. 2d 392, 406 (1980). *Forrester v. White, 484 U.S. at 227-229, 108 S. Ct. at 54-55 (1987); Westfall v Erwin, 108 S. Ct. 580 (1987); United States v. Lanier (March 1997).*

The Fourteenth Amendment prohibits a state [federal] from denying any person [citizen] within its jurisdiction the equal protection under the laws. Since a State [or federal] acts only by its legislative, executive or judicial authorities, the constitutional provisions must be addressed to those authorities, including state and federal judges . . ."

Scheeler v. City of St. Cloud, 402 F 3d 826, 830 (8th circuit 2005) Title 18 U.S.C 242. Deprivation of rights under color of law. Whoever, under color of any law, statue, ordinance, regulation, or custom, willfully subject any person . . . to the deprivation of any rights, privileges, or immunities secured or protected by the Constitution or laws of the United States, or to different punishment, pains, or penalties, on account of such person being an alien or by reason of his color, or race, than are prescribed for the punishment of citizens, shall be fined under this title or imprisoned not more than one year, or both.

Finally, one must take into account the long history of harassment and retaliation against Appellant Fearing as exemplified in previous court documents in appeal Case No. 06-2300, Case No. 06-4078, (Judge Ericksen was assigned to both cases in district court) and the egregious and unlawful conduct by Defendants in how they conspired to evict the Doe family, simply because their children were black; and the joint efforts by all parties acting "Under the Color" of law to violate Appellant's Constitutional Rights. And now we have a federal judge (Judge Joan Ericksen) condoning and sanctioning such conduct by denying and blocking Appellants right to due process under the law.

Dated: June 13, 2008
Signed: Marlene Fearing

*   *   *

This is American Justice today, folks. Unless you had a court experience recently or know of someone who has, the majority of the American public are simply not aware of the corruption taking place in our judicial process. There is no "Rule of Law". There is no "Constitution". Some of these judges think they are bigger than God. Clearly the courts are used for political retribution as my cases are perfect examples of that. The appellate courts across America have been stacked with neo-con judges thanks to George W. Bush and his Republican Congress. How many times have we heard George Bush say, "I want judges in the courts that uphold and rule by the Constitution". Sounds good, Mr. President, but who's Constitution were you speaking of—Chinas? Because, what happened to the black family and me has no resemblance to the U.S. Constitution.

My understanding of our Judicial process is that justice is administered according to the "Rule of Law", the Constitution and the evidence. What we have today is judicial rulings based on party line ideology, political retribution and the Constitution is non-existent. We need to hold our elected officials responsible for this travesty—enough with the lies.

How can an American have their home taken from them because of their ethnicity under U.S. Constitutional law? How can a developer that upholds fair housing laws in America have all of her assets taken from her because she refused to violate State and Federal housing laws? That is not upholding the U.S. Constitution, Mr. Bush. That is called Constitutional tyranny!

Today it was the family of blacks and I that obviously have no Constitutional Rights when we had our homes and assets taken from us; and stripped of our civil liberties. *Tomorrow it could be you, a member of your family or your neighbor. Where and when will it stop? It will only stop when we as Americans take back our country.*

TAKING BACK AMERICA

Under the Bush Administration, I feel that we have lost our moral authority in terms of how our Country is perceived not only by its own citizens, but other Nations as well. As an American Citizen, where do you go to seek help and protection when those elected and sworn to uphold and defend the Constitution are the very ones who are committing treasonous acts against America? **If we are a nation of laws, why are they not upheld when it is government that is the perpetrator? And why are they allowed to break the law with impunity?**

What happened to our Democracy? The Democratic process is supposed to work for everyone. My experiences tell me that it works best for those with wealth and power and those who are politically well-connected.

There's a lot of truth in the adage, "If you don't use it—you lose it." Well, America, we lost it! Our silence, indifference and apathy in allowing our politicians and politically appointed neo-con judges, to take free rein has steered us into the abyss. I am equally as guilty because I also trusted that the system worked. My documentary is proof that our system only works, when as Americans, we all make it work by our participation and involvement. As Americans, we can no longer sit on the side-lines as spectators. We must all become involved and proactive in taking back our country before we have complete anarchy. I am in complete agreement with Bill Moyers, for Common Dreams:

"Democracy in America is a series of narrow escapes and we may be running out of luck. The reigning presumption about the American experience, as the historian Lawrence Goodwyn has written, is grounded in the idea of progress, the conviction that the present is 'better' than

the past and the future will bring even more improvement. For all of its short-comings, we keep telling ourselves, 'The system works.' Now all bets are off. We have fallen under the spell of money, faction, and fear, and the great American experience in creating a different future together has been subjugated to individual cunning in the pursuit of wealth and power—and to the claims of empire, with its ravenous demands and stuporous distractions."

Government reports indicate that the cost to educate a child is $8,000. per year. The cost to house and feed a prisoner is $32,000. per year. So why is it that we tend to opt for more prisons and incarceration as opposed to education and rehabilitation? For a country that espouses to place such a high value on human life this is a frightening and abominable contradiction, when we would rather subjugate our citizens to a life of suffering rather than to a life of fulfillment and enjoyment.

Our elected officials frequently criticize civil rights abuses of foreign countries—as if our record were free of sin—and yet I was incarcerated for protesting civil rights violations here in America. How do we rationalize that dichotomy? Incarceration seems to be the answer to all of our problems. The very fact that today the United States of America has over two million of its citizens (mostly non-violent) incarcerated along with violent offenders so they can learn—what? How to become a real criminal and that's our perpetuating cycle with the prison system. That should raise some questions as to whether we really are a "Free Democratic Society" or has it become a means of dealing with minorities since most incarcerated are non-white.

We can no longer ignore the fact that there is a different justice system for whites than for people of color or as in my case, anyone who defends them. We incarcerate more of our citizens than the entire world put together. In my opinion that doesn't speak well for a Country that espouses freedom and Democracy for all people. It is not my intent to be divisive or confrontational; it is simply a fact that we as a Nation need to address, sooner rather than later. We cannot fix the problems if we don't identify them by an honest assessment. And this Documentary does just that—identifies *some* of the culprits and underhanded tactics by governmental officials on America's payroll.

I am convinced that what is taking place today in our government, and what happened to me and the black family would not have happened under the Clinton Administration for two reasons: 1.) Under Janet Reno's U.S. Justice Department, they did the right thing in grabbing the City by the throat when they froze their funds. That took courage. They would not have done that if there wasn't sufficient evidence to show illegal conduct on the part of the City and efforts made to end such conduct. (It was Bush's U.S. Justice Department that sanctioned the City's conduct when they closed the file when Bush became elected) 2.) The judicial system was not yet stacked with neo-con judges that abuse their power and refuse to acknowledge the existence of the U.S. Constitution. That all happened under Bush and his Republican Congress. It's a sad day for America when judges are used for political retribution and retaliation against a U.S. Citizen for speaking out against government corruption.

What happened to me is a perfect example of how corruption in government is accomplished—no checks or balances and those with absolute power use their political positions to punish those who are not in agreement or foes of their accomplices. Corruption in our system is not new, but in my case, I've wondered many times as to how widely spread and how far up the ladder this kind of corruption reaches? From information that I have gathered, the answer is quite far when the judicial process is complicit at even the federal level. I thought my story was unique, but in checking on the internet it seems such horrors are experienced all over this Country, but they go unreported by the news media. That then begs the question—do we really have free press? Perhaps the "free press" is not so free after all.

I have contacted many news outlets and reported this story. Several showed an interest and did investigate, but when they discovered that it was the government acting as criminals, they decided that they were fearful that they would become embroiled in a protracted and costly legal battle. Others answered that "this is not the type of story that they report". An investigator from the St. Paul Pioneer Press investigated this story for months, but when it came time to file the report, the Editor refused to print it. City Pages in Minneapolis wrote an article, but the majority of it was distorted and had no resemblance to the truth. One Nation News also did an article, and they were much closer to the truth, but due to limitation on print space it was not as in depth as it should have been for the public to really get a sense of how broken our government really is.

In looking at the positive side, perhaps it's a 'good thing' that the "Supremes" gave us George W. Bush as President in 2000. How else would America have gotten a taste of what it is like to live under a "Dictatorship"? In my opinion, this man has obliterated our Constitution and brought such disgrace and dishonor to our Country—all under the pretext of keeping us safe. How is ignoring the existence of the constitution, stacking the courts with right wing neo-con judges (that abuse their power) and other civil rights abuses directed at the American people keeping us safe? His medicine is worse than the ailment. And where has congress been, both Democrats and Republicans—boys and girls hired by the American People to represent our best interests?

Yes, there are people trying to kill Americans. But, I think it might be wise if we first identify the enemy before we drop bombs. How is attacking a foreign country—unprovoked, spying on Americans; and trashing our Constitution and freedoms keeping us safe? Just maybe we need to put our own house in order. I think that we should consider Mr. Bush and his right-winged colleagues as a wake-up call to America. America is in dire need of some drastic changes; and I believe high on the priority list should be holding "Rogue Judges" accountable for their conduct. These people are appointed for life and some (as I have experienced) use their own personal agendas and violate the "Rule of Law". They are on the American Payroll to implement their own agenda and to hell with the Constitution and the "Rule of Law". If Congress can hire them, they can also fire them through an impeachment process.

Is this being disrespectful to the judiciary as a whole? I think not. I believe the good judges who follow the "Rule of Law" would welcome such a move. I think most judges, both Democrat and Republican are repulsed by what's taking place. It brings dishonor to all of them. I personally would like to see respect and dignity once again for the judicial process. That has been lost recently. I remain positive and hopeful that America will rise to the occasion as it always does. Because it's the American people that make America so great.

Recent newspaper articles have accused me of being a "troublemaker" and a "martyr" for defending a cause. I am neither. The only 'cause' I have is that *I am an ordinary American* who is fed up with the "Pretty Lies" that our leaders are force feeding us. If I am a "martyr" and a "troublemaker", then I think we need more; then just maybe we might have less government corruption. While I am being punished, demonized and portrayed as unpatriotic, I feel that quite the opposite is true. I was raised to believe that first and foremost, you obey the laws, you love your neighbor, your Country and to show compassion for your fellow man. Am I perfect? Far from it. I've lost both shoes and have probably sinned more in my heart than one of my favorite American Presidents. However, I find it more gratifying to pull someone up when they are in need, instead of kicking them to the curb.

This entire process by the authorities is to assassinate my character. Since they don't like that I speak the truth they attempt to redefine me to justify their assaults against me. Evidence will show that I have been tormented, taunted and pushed to the brink and still I refused to succumb to their attacks and threats. When people learn of my story, they ask me, why I didn't purchase a gun to protect myself from such assaults, when police refused to give me protection? The thought occurred to me, but I realized that, that is exactly what they want me to do. They would like for me to respond in violence in protecting myself, but not one of those "Hate Merchants" are worth spending the rest of my life in prison. I will admit that I have never understood how people can become violent, however, now I have a clear understanding as to how that can happen—when you are unjustly attacked (by those who should be defending you) to the point that you feel hopeless and helpless with no end in sight as fear and terror surrounds you—that's how.

I believe that defending our way of life can be accomplished without violence. And that is exactly what I intend to do. My journal will be my weapon in exposing those responsible for the assault on our Constitution and civil liberties. Exposing these tyrants will be the best vindication for me. **At this point, it makes no difference to me that these "Haters" are powerful and influential. After 15 years of attacks, I have moved beyond fear. I believe that there is a much bigger Judge that will have the final word in this matter.**

We don't challenge those in power because of either fear of retaliation, or knowing full well that as one person—alone; we don't stand a prayer of a chance to change anything by protesting or confronting them. How many preceded me and received similar treatment by Minnesota government is anyone's guess as nobody's talking because they are either *sufficiently stigmatized* or *unable*.

I believe that there was a point in time that we could trust our Minnesota government, but not anymore, since the elitists have taken control. A little glimpse into that is the flap over the replacement of Minnesota U.S. Attorney Heffelfinger. He was the attorney that showed an interest in protecting voting rights of Minnesota's Native Americans. Supposedly, Mr. Heffelfinger resigned, but according to a L.A. Times report his neck was on the chopping block at U.S. Justice in D.C. like other U.S. Attorneys that were fired for trying to enforce the law. Even though Mr. Heffelfinger was Republican, apparently his interest in upholding the law as a U. S. Attorney was in conflict with Bush's controlled U.S. Justice Department so they found a Bush loyalist to replace him. Based on testimony at recent 'Hearings' by congress regarding such matters, attorneys being hired and promoted at the U.S. Justice Department were given priority based on their loyalty to Bush and more qualified attorneys were passed over because of their political affiliation.

Minnesota has lost its goodness when we lost the likes of Hubert Humphrey and Paul Wellstone. They fought for equality and truly were interested in serving all Minnesotans. I think that Governor Jesse Ventura tried, but he met with much resistance and a lack of cooperation on both sides. The news media certainly didn't help matters. We have since had nobody to champion for the rights of those disenfranchised by the system. Both Senators, Norm Coleman, a Republican and Senator Amy Klobucher, a Democrat were made aware of the corruption, but they have chosen to ride the gravy train rather than dirty themselves in attempting to clean up this mess. Both have taken the position that the judiciary is another branch of government that they can't intervene in and the U.S. Justice Department is under the authority of the Presidency. Apparently they are not even aware of their roles as senators, (their power to conduct congressional hearings, their power to legislate or to impeach judges who commit crimes against the U.S. Government).

Should an American be subjected to such trauma and terror as the family of blacks and I have been subjected to because of racist, sexist attitudes in this Country? It was our government—State and Federal that orchestrated this travesty—starting with a local State Judge and City Mayor, his corrupt judicial colleagues, to State and then Federal Government. All of them, locking arms in trying to cover up their corrupt conduct. I refused to cooperate, so I became the "Problem" that wouldn't go away. That's what this is all about.

This is the "Real World" of trying to do business legally with a corrupt government that allows and supports racism, sexism and retaliation, using "fear" tactics as I have experienced. This is how our system works behind the scenes in Minnesota. Again, ***I challenge anyone to prove me wrong***.

In writing this documentary, it became a self-reflective journey inward for me—The purpose for my existence and my role as a human being, a mother, a grandmother, a citizen of America and a citizen of this world. I came to the realization that this was not just about me because everything that was happening was for a reason that was much bigger than me. I had always chosen the path of least resistance—yet trying to make positive changes without a lot of hoopla. But that all changed for me when by first hand experiences I found such unacceptable behavior in America, a Nation that espouses to be a "Champion for human rights". I could not live with myself if I did nothing to stop the madness that surrounded me so I just let my heart lead the way.

After all of these years of being subjected to the "politics of fear" by government officials including judges who demonstrated their absolute abuse of power, while I had none—how do I find justice? I could not find justice when my Constitutional Rights are non—existent under such a corrupt and broken system. This "wrong" can only be made "right" by the American people in voting these "bums" out of office. I had no power against such a corrupt and formidable force. I believe, however, that "Good" can come from something this "Evil" and I do have the power to make that happen. I have set up a trust fund to donate monies generated from the book sales to my favorite charities. God Bless All!

Marlena Fearing

AFTER WORD

My documentary was to be published and ready for market in September, 2008, prior to the election of November, 2008. It is now one year later, August, 2009. Given the provocative and controversial nature of my book, it has met with much resistance. For various excuses and reasoning my book could not be available for market until recently. Subsequently some events were written in past tense and slightly outdated, but all events remain truthful and forthright in content.

Recent update is that Barack Obama was elected President and I shall keep an open mind and remain optimistic that his justice department will defend the Constitution.

Thus far, it remains business as usual in Minnesota at least in the Valley of Evil from Hastings on up to Stillwater. In an earlier chapter, I outlined the "whitewashing" taking place in Washington County by Richard Ilka. He was the prosecutor for the City of Oakdale that was chosen to cover-up the wrongdoings of Robert Swenson and Attorney Jon Kingstad. Mr. Ilka was rewarded for his evil deeds. He is now a judge in Washington County District Court. So it's business as usual at the Washington County Court House in Stillwater, MN. Evil once again is rewarded.

The same is true for Dakota County in Hastings, Minnesota. The City Attorney, Shawn Moynihan, that aided in drafting fraudulent documents and then committed perjury in court to cover for his conduct has also been rewarded for his evil ways by becoming a State District Court Judge. Bad behavior also pays off in Hastings, MN. Nothing will change in Minnesota until they elect a State Attorney General with a back bone that will uphold the law and protect the Citizens of that State from such corruption.

It appears that the necessary ingredient to become a judge in either of these counties is to prove capacity and ability to ignore the laws of the land. Heaven help the poor soul who seeks justice before either of these men if they are anything other than Caucasian!

TESTIMONIALS

I have set aside an entire chapter to include excerpts from letters and affidavits from those who have witnessed more of the conduct by the City, their planners, the attorneys involved and judges involved in these cases.

AFFIDAVIT OF THEODOR PERLINGER:

1. I have known Ms. Marlene Fearing since 1991. She constructed my home in Afton, MN. I have never met a more honest, ethical and principled lady than Ms. Fearing. When I heard that she was contemplating developing St. Croix Villas, I had a great interest in buying one of her twinhomes because it fit my lifestyle much better since I traveled a lot in my business.
2. Because I was interested in what she was proposing, I went to quite a few of the Council Meetings at Lake St. Croix Beach. I was appalled at the hostility directed at Ms. Fearing by the City, particularly City Attorney Mark Vierling and Mayor John Jansen.
3. I recall one meeting (earlier stage) that was quite memorable. Ms. Fearing's attorney Bob Dickie was also present. The attitude and conduct at this meeting by the City was even more confrontational than in the past. It appeared to me that the City simply did not want to cooperate with Ms. Fearing.
4. After the meeting, Mayor Jansen approached Ms. Fearing and stated, "Let me warn you, Ms. Fearing, if you plan to sue like you did in Hastings, I know every Judge in this County."
5. I was shocked that a Mayor would conduct himself in such a threatening manner.

Signed and notarized on March 18, 2002
By Theodor Perlinger

AFFIDAVIT OF ROBERT NUIS

Robert Nuis, a resident of the County of Pima, State of Arizona, being duly sworn states as follows:

1. That Iowa is my primary residence; however I reside in Arizona as well as Minnesota during the summer and fall of 2003 and 2004.
2. That I have knowledge of many of the transactions conducted by Marlene Fearing's representatives, mainly her attorney Mark Kallenbach, Dennis Gauthier and Ron Nechodom of GNA and A-Z Group (hired to collect on her $600,000. Judgment against the Aymar Group) Michael Aymar, Transaction Real Estate, Minnesota Real Estate Specialists and LSCBCO, LLC.
3. That I attended many meetings and court appearances of which I was instructed by Ms. Fearing to take copious notes which the following **is a** brief summarization of what took place. I am also reporting other information that was relayed to me by other witnesses to the various events.
4. That GNA (Dennis Gauthier, Ron Nechodom and Ross Anderson) was the investigative team that Ms. Fearing hired shortly after her judgment against the Aymar Group. Ms. Fearing gave Mr. Gauthier full Power of attorney to do all things necessary to assist her in all of her legal matters, including hiring and firing attorneys to represent her in the discrimination claim against the City as well as collection of the $600,000. Judgment, Initiating a Receivership, collection of $150,000. from a State Recovery Fund (Commerce Dept.) as part of judgment on Aymar's E&O as a licensed real estate broker, and collecting on properties and assets of Aymar.
5. That initially Mr. Gauthier hired Mark Kallenbach to handle her federal discrimination case as time was of the essence since many of her claims would be lost if not timely filed.
6. That I was present during that initial first meeting with Mark Kallenbach and all those subsequent. The very first meeting was held in early the October, 2003, at the Bungalow in Lakeland, MN. Mr. Kallenbach made no commitment to take the case at that time, but stated that he was extremely interested since his case load was fairly minimal at the time and that it sounded of great interest to him.

7. That we met again for the second time at Ms. Fearing's home toward the end of October. Present at the meeting were Ms. Fearing, Dennis Gauthier, Ron Nechodom, Mark Kallenbach and his wife Michelle and myself. At this meeting Ms. Fearing forewarned Mr. Kallenbach about the difficulty in presenting this case and the power of the City and the League of Cities and their methods of smoke screening their wrongdoings with volumes of documents. To that Mr. Kallenbach stated," He knew all of the law firms including City attorney Vierling and that he was aware they would bury him with a truckload of documents, of which perhaps only 3 of the documents would incriminate the City. Then I went to Ms. Fearing's office and came back with a huge binder which neatly outlined and organized all the issues, affidavits of witness, various rulings by HUD and the Minnesota Department of Human Rights. Upon review of the documents Mr. Kallenbach stated to Ms. Fearing, "You've already got the case mostly prepared so all I have to do is research and apply the laws, but you must do the typing". Ms. Fearing agreed. Mr. Kallenbach verbally agreed to take the case. Ms. Fearing asked for a time frame as she was in a cash flow bind and Mr. Kallenbach repeatedly stated to Ms. Fearing, "I only eat what I kill" and finally explained that he doesn't charge unless he collects.

8. That at this same meeting Mr. Kallenbach was told of the other issues involving Mary Parr, Bob Swenson and how they were attempting to collect on Ms. Fearing's judgment by bringing in a frivolous lawsuit claiming that the project had been represented as a senior community. To that Mr. Kallenbach stated. "Their (Parr/Swenson) party will soon be over as he intended to bring an immediate TRO against them. That never happened. And neither did he prepare or file any case in federal court against the City. Ms. Fearing as told by Dennis Gauthier in March of 2004 that Mark Kallenbach decided not to take the case because he was more interested in taking over from attorney Tom White on the collection of the $600,000 Judgment. In fact, Mr. Kallenbach posed this question to Ms. Fearing at one meeting, "This will be a slam dunk, and I hope you won't be upset with me for only putting in about 10 hours of legal work for a $120,000 fee". To that Ms. Fearing stated to Dennis Gauthier that if Mark just took the gravy of the judgment, nobody would take the federal case. However, Kallenbach stated that he would find somebody to take the federal case. That never happened.

9. That by the time Ms. Fearing got the news from Kallenbach that he would not take the federal case, most of her issues had been lost because of statute of limitations prohibiting her from recovery of business losses of $1.6 million dollars.

10. That in March, 2004, there was a meeting at the Perkins Restaurant on Riverside Ave., Mpls. In attendance were Ms. Fearing, Mr. Kallenbach, Mr. Gauthier, Mr. Nechodom, Mr. Doran, and myself. The purpose of this meeting was to establish how the collection of assets in the judgment against the Aymar Group would proceed and who would be responsible for the collection on the vacant lots. Even though lots 1, 2, 3 and 13 were named as assets to be collected upon as outlined in Ms. Fearing's legal contract with Mr. Kallenbach, it was established that those lots essentially still belonged to Ms. Fearing in fee simple title as she had not been paid for them by Aymar. Mr. Kallenbach asked Mr. Doran to collect on all the lots 1,2,3, 6, 8. 12, and 19 and he would pay him, but to keep the fees down. Then it was discovered that lots 1, 2 and 3 were still owned by Ms. Fearing as fee simple owner. The legal fees were to be paid to Jim Doran on those three lots by Ms Fearing. Mr. Kallenbach could then focus on only lots 6, 8, 12 and 19. Attorney Chad Lemmons was to seek quiet title action on lot 13, which comprised of Ms. Fearing's home that was being foreclosed on by a bank that Aymar fraudulently acquired a mortgage on.

11. That issues of importance at yet another meeting at Perkins was that attorney James Doran repeatedly told Mr.Kallenbach that under no circumstances was he to do anything other than ask for a jury trial in the matter of Parr/Swenson. That there has been a pattern of judicial abuse in all of Ms. Fearing's cases and Mr. Doran told of how judges would rule against Ms. Fearing even when evidence supported her case. He told of how Judge Cass in his presence asked Ms. Fearing to visit with him in the privacy of his chamber without counsel and on another time Judge Cass ruled that she pay a mechanic lien holder even though he acknowledged that he made a mistake and that Ms. Fearing had actually already overpaid him. Judge Cass ordered Ms. Fearing to pay him again as well as all of his legal expenses and attorney fees. Mr. Doran also indicated that Mr. Kallenbach should file against Judge Carlson in the Parr/Swenson case as she was even worse than Judge Cass.

12. That at the end of March, 2004, even though attorney Tom White (previous attorney that handled the Parr/Swenson case prior to Mr. Kallenbach taking over) filed for a Jury trial, Judge Carlson had not paneled a jury and Mr. Kingstad wasn't ready for trial. Judge Carlson after stating openly in court that, "I don't want to hear anything about discrimination because this City is too small" even though the City was never named in the lawsuit as plaintiff, but the Judge essentially acknowledged that Parr/Swenson are the City's agents. Judge Carlson goes on to say, "Mr. Kallenbach I am sure that you will appeal my decision". She admits that she has made a decision prior to seeing any evidence. Judge Carlson then asked to see attorneys Kingstad and Kallenbach in her chambers. Mark Kallenbach's wife, Michelle was allowed to also attend this meeting. The significance of this meeting is as follows:

   A. Judge Carlson told Mr. Kallenbach that she didn't like his client (Fearing).
   B. Michelle stressed that point repeatedly, "she really hates you Marlene".
   C. Instead of a jury trial, Mr. Kallenbach asks for a Summary Judgment even though the judge just told him that she was ruling against Ms. Fearing. This is exactly what Mr. Doran told him "not to do" as it would prejudice Ms. Fearing's case because there were too many issues and facts involved that needed to be decided by an impartial jury and not by a Judge who has already admitted her intense disliking of Ms. Fearing. Even Chad Lemmons told Mr.Kallenbach that there appears to be a problem for Ms. Fearing to get impartial and fair judicial findings in Washington County Court. For Mr. Lemmons to make such an acknowledgment is really saying something.

13. That in May, 2004, the hearing for Summary Judgment took place, while Mr. Kingstad, argued for his clients close to an hour or more. When it came time for Mr. Kallenbach, he stood up and told the judge that this is a very emotional case and that she should read his brief. So rather than a zealous defense, there was no defense. It is my strong belief that it is Mark's wife that writes all the briefs for him, because he has no knowledge of the contents of the brief. When Judge Carlson asked him a question he turned around and looked at Ms. Fearing and

holds his hands in the air. This was so typical in every court hearing.
Mr. Kallenbach appeared clueless. Mr. Kingstad again repeats more
of their perjured testimony of his clients Parr/Swenson, he attacks
Ms. Fearing in a vile manner characterizing her as a liar, incorrigible,
litigious, etc. essentially accusing Ms. Fearing of everything that he and
his clients were guilty of. It was pure character assassination and Mr.
Kallenbach said nothing in Ms. Fearing's defense. He could have at
least pointed out that in terms of litigious, it was in fact Mr. Kingstad
that was initiating all of the litigation, in terms of dishonesty, it was
Parr/Swenson who lied to the courts that they had standing to bring
litigation when in fact they did not. However, most importantly, not
ever did Mr. Kallenbach point out that all evidence supports Ms.
Fearing's contentions that she had sold to people of all ages even those
with children and not once did Parr/Swenson complain about ages or
children until the occupants were black. Judge Carlson stated openly
in court "I will take this case under advisement but I can tell you Mr.
Kallenbach your client has 11 cases too many". There are no 11 cases,
a complete exaggeration. In her findings, she acknowledges that Mr.
Kalllenbach did not challenge the age issues or much of other false
evidence presented by Kingstad. There were many affidavits submitted
by residents to the judge that supported Ms. Fearing, from ages of
people to the fact that Kingstad and his clients had no standing to
bring litigation against Ms. Fearing. Not once did Mr. Kallenbach
offer this crucial evidence in support of Ms. Fearing's case. He acted
as if it didn't exist. Bottom line, all favorable evidence in support of
Ms. Fearing did not even become part of court records, because Mr.
Kallenbach didn't think it was necessary. I spoke to many people who
attended the hearing and I heard repeatedly that Ms. Fearing would
have been much better off had she had no legal counsel because Mr.
Kallenbach hurt her with his incompetence. A comment made by
Ron Nechodom, one of the individuals responsible for hiring Mark
Kallenbach, fairly sums up Mr. Kallenbach's performance by stating,
"Well, Mark got his ass handed to him, which supports the above
that he was never organized, or prepared and had no knowledge of
what his brief contained.

14. That after the Hearing Kallenbach waves and yells at Kingstad in
the court corridors, "I'm filing a Rule 11 Mr. Kingstad". No such
ruling was ever filed. It is my understanding that Ms. Fearing has
filed such a motion to be heard by Judge Armstrong, but it has been

delayed due to the appeals. So essentially Kingstad was successful in getting a judgment of $33,000. in attorney fees against Ms. Fearing and another $23,000. Judgment against Ms. Fearing for bogus fees supposedly owed to the Association. Even though it was acknowledged to me by Tony Thooft, the President of the the present Association, that it was the Association that owed Ms. Fearing some $28,500. rather than the other way around. Mr. Kallenbach never presented this information to the courts as the documentation was still in the hands of Mary Parr as former Secretary/Treasurer and she refused to relinquish it. Rather than asking the courts to intervene to acquire this important documentation supporting Ms. Fearing, Mr. Kallenbach just ignored it and as he did in so much other evidence that supported Ms. Fearing.

15. That given the demeanor of the Judge and comments that she made in the court room that we already knew the outcome without her taking anything under advisement. After the findings by Judge Carlson, Mark Kallenbach just disappeared. Ms. Fearing called him repeatedly and wrote to him via the email and he refused to answer her. This went on for months. I could see Ms. Fearing's health deteriorating. She would be bedridden for days with headaches, heart palpations and stomach ailments. Ms. Fearing ended up in the hospital for almost a week with heart problems. I then took it upon myself to contact Dennis Gauthier and Ron Nechodom in support of Ms. Fearing to find out where Kallenbach was and had he done anything on the appeal. It is my feelings that had Kallenback done what he promised to do in the first place by having a jury trial rather than jeopardizing Ms Fearing's case with a judge who admitted she didn't like Ms. Fearing, this wouldn't have happened. Failure to protect his client, Ms. Fearing enables his fees from approximately $30,000 to over $125,000 with ongoing litigation. Kallenbach's behavior in how he treated Ms. Fearing is absolutely inexcusable. When an attorney causes more stress for his client, than the case itself is gross neglect and incompetence in the most egregious form.

16. That during this time frame, I communicated to Gauthier and Nechodom that Ms. Fearing had a buyer for Lot 12. (Property that Kallenbach agreed to collect on at the March, 2003 meeting, as property secretly owned by Aymar). Gauthier and Nechodom indicated that they would get Kallenbach to take care of getting that lot with the house, released from the attorney representing

the mortgage company. Instead of negotiating for the release of the property, the attorney representing the mortgage company hung up on Kallenbach when he called him a ***sucker. This was acknowledged by Gauthier and Nechodom as Kallenbach boasted how he told this guy off. This is another typical Kallenbach "ego trip" that did nothing to benefit Ms. Fearing, the investigators or himself as no monies were collected.

17. That Ms. Fearing repeatedly stressed to Gauthier, Nechodom and Kallenbach that she had difficulty financially and could they please do something on the receivership to collect monies or on property that Aymar had fraudulently transferred, lots 6, 8, 12, and 19. Mr. Kallenbach stated that he could possibly get a loan for Ms. Fearing but the rate would be 3% per month. "This is something Kallenback told me personally at the Perkins meeting in March 2004. It turned out that the party interested in making the loan at an annual rate of 36% (slightly usurious) was an associate and partner of Kallenbach's. Gauthier contacted me and said that he had a buyer for the lots of which he wanted 20% for himself and then another 20% for Kallenbach on a sale purported to be $600,000. My answer was that since Mr. Kallenbach did no legal work to clear title, but rather all legal work was done by James Doran who was subsequently paid by Ms. Fearing. When I asked if these were his buyers or Mr. Kallenbach's, Gauthier stated that they were his buyers. Later, it was disclosed by Gauthier's partner Nechodom, that the interested buyer was indeed an associate of Kallenbach's, however, he didn't want anyone knowing that because it would be a conflict in an attorney/client relationship. But what I found out during this process was that clearly Kallenbach's interest was not in the best interest of his client, Marlene Fearing, but rather Mark Kallenbach's wallet.

18. That during the litigation with Parr/Swenson, Ms. Fearing and I were told by GNA that the collection of the $600,000. had to be put on the back burner and that Kallenbach had agreed to do the Parr/Swenson case pro bono to protect the judgment. This was repeated to me repeatedly by Gauthier and Nechodom that this was pro bono. It was obvious in the various court hearings that the Parr/Swenson lawsuit was merely a ruse to remove the blacks from the development and at the same time collect on all of Ms. Fearing's assets and land. *At one hearing, Kingstad filed a motion to have Ms. Fearing held in contempt of court for writing a letter defending the Hall family.*

Kingstad told the Judge that he wanted Ms. Fearing incarcerated until she agrees to give up all of her real estate holdings and then they want her run out of town for good. Mr. Kallenbach, once again said absolutely nothing in Ms. Fearing's defense. He just stood there and said nothing.

19. That during all the above, Michael Aymar filed for personal bankruptcy. However, all the evidence collected by GNA during their investigation showed that Mr. Aymar was collecting between $200,000-300,000. through his various bank accounts and businesses. Mr. Kallenbach knew that Mr. Aymar was committing a fraud on the bankruptcy court, but he filed absolutely nothing to have him removed out of bankruptcy court. However, he kept telling Ms. Fearing and I that he was going to make such a demand to the bankruptcy trustee. He did no such thing. Instead he calls for a deposition of Mr. Aymar, by the trustee. Once again Aymar offers perjured testimony the third time relative to his income and Kallenbach makes a comment that "He feels sorry for the poor bastard" and offered him a name of a good criminal attorney. With this kind of evidence that clearly showed fraud, Mr. Kallenbach again is negligent in protecting his client, Ms. Fearing.

20. That I wrote to the bankruptcy court and asked for an explanation as to how Mr. Aymar could repeatedly offer perjured testimony and the trustee allows him a discharge. A district investigator (Fokkena) from the Bankruptcy court called Ms. Fearing as well as myself and indicated that had Mr. Kallenbach filed documentation of fraud and other supporting evidence to the bankruptcy court, Mr. Aymar would not have been given a discharge and Ms. Fearing could be collecting on her judgment. Fokkena repeatedly asked, "Why didn't Ms. Fearing's attorney do anything for her?" He indicated that it was not the Trustee's duty to act in Ms. Fearing's behalf, but rather the duty of her attorney Mr. Kallenbach to file proper documentation.

21. That Mr. Kallenbach also took over the Receivership Case to collect on the $600,000 Judgment which had been already initiated by attorney Tom White. According to Mr. Kallenbach, Mr. White had filed for the receivership using incorrect statutes, therefore, he would have to terminate the receivership after 3 months of collecting nothing, but he would refile using appropriate statutes. This entire case is an absolute mystery as to how some $200,000-300,000. to

flow through the accounts and not collect a dime during a 3 month receivership. By Gauthier's own admission, there were three bank accounts at the time the receivership was put in place and $66,000 in one account which Gauthier indicate that he would have released to Ms.Fearing immediately. That never happened. It was clear from the 2 to 3 meetings we had with GNA that Mr. Kallenbach was very much involved in this receivership. Ms. Fearing has repeatedly asked for an accounting of all the bank accounts but only one was provided which clearly depicts some questionable transactions, i.e. Mr. Aymar was allowed to pay out of his business account for, porn materials from a fantasy adult shop, child custody and spousal support payments, all of his entertainment expenses, his boat expenses and other unrelated personal expenses by charging it off as business expenses. By Gauthier's own admission, the receiver, GNA partner (Ross Anderson) was aiding and abetting Mr. Aymar's efforts to steal from the receivership by helping him draft false documents to justify the withdrawals, i.e. phony bills by fictitious suppliers or playing the usual identity switch through another brother working at a subsidiary firm. Since Mr. Kallenbach at this point in time, had taken over as attorney of record from Tom White, and he was fully aware of all the information supplied by the investigators to Ms. Fearing and I. Again he did nothing to remove the receiver or protect the assets to satisfy the judgment awarded to Ms. Fearing.

22. That in the 2 years that I have been a witness to this entire fiasco, I feel that Ms. Fearing would have been far better off today without any so called legal counsel. I was under the impression in all professional functions; a lawyer should be competent, prompt, and diligent in his zealous defense of his client. From what I have observed Mr. Kallenbach has some real issues to resolve, personally as well as professionally. If there is one thing that is most obvious with Mr. Kallenbach is his vulgarity and giant "ego". His incompetence is depicted in the events as stated above, not to mention the serious financial and health results inflicted upon Ms. Fearing by this gross negligence.

Notarized and
Signed by Robert N. Nuis

*		*		*

March 11, 2004

Sgt. Gary Swanson
Washington County Sheriff's Department
Washington County Government Center
14949 N 62nd St.
Stillwater, MN 55082

Re: ICR # 103043368 (Mary Parr)

Dear Sgt. Swanson:

I am writing as a follow-up to our conversation of yesterday. The above documented complaint indicates that on Thanksgiving Day, November 27, 2003, Mary Parr with the aid of her juvenile grandson took a chainsaw to my marketing signs. The original cost of those signs which was done in 1994,was approximately $6,000. The cost to replace them today is $8,173.88 (See Attached Invoice) I think we are in agreement, that this is considered a felony. Now as to my understanding of the chain of events, from our conversation, is that subsequent to my filing a complaint against Mary Parr for theft and destruction of my marketing signs, the complaint was submitted to the City for prosecution. The City refused to prosecute, so I insisted that the complaint be submitted to Washington County for prosecution. Washington County also refused to prosecute and deemed the act a civil matter, due to extenuating circumstances. Those extenuating circumstances being that the City authorized the destruction of my signs. *This is not civil, this is criminal!*

It is my position that Mary Parr, nor the City of Lake St. Croix Beach are above the law. I have spoken with Officer Engel this morning and have requested that my complaint be amended to include the City for conspiring to commit a felony. Those signs have been up since 1994 with City approval. Those signs belonged to me. Nobody had my permission to remove or destroy them. I am requesting that this be sent back to Washington County Attorney's office for prosecution. If this is considered to be a conflict because the perpetrator of a crime is another local governmental entity, then perhaps this file should be submitted to the State Attorney Generals Office for prosecution.

Thank you for your cooperation in this matter. I look forward to hearing from you soon.

Sincerely,
Marlene Fearing

*   *   *

April 1, 2004

Office of Governor Tim Pawlenty
130 State Capital
75 Dr. Martin Luther King Blvd.
St. Paul, MN 55155

FAX: 651-296-2089

Re: MDHR—Housing Discrimination

Dear Governor Pawlenty:

Thank you for requesting that MDHR Commissioner Ms. Korbel reply to my letter of November 15, 2003. I have responded to her letter today of which I am forwarding a copy as well to you. While Ms. Korbel denies my allegations that both the Cities of Hastings and Lake St. Croix Beach violated Fair Housing laws, my rebuttal and attached affidavits tell quite a different story from people in the know (Mayors who witnessed the discrimination).

I am requesting that an investigation be conducted as to why my rights were not protected when I refused to participate with the two aforementioned Cities in their efforts to implement unfair and illegal housing practices. Ms. Korbel acknowledges the lengthy duration and she's correct. But the reason it is still on going is because no enforcing agency, for whatever reason, has made any effort to stop them. I personally have had to endure the wrath of retaliation by both Cities for telling them that their housing policies violate Federal and State Housing Laws. It's up to the MDHR to do that, not me. What happened to me is an outrage and I believe the public needs to know, particularly those who have also been aggrieved by such housing violations.

Thank you in advance for your interest in this matter.

Sincerely,
Marlene Fearing

*   *   *

Mr. Theodore Perlinger
1470 Quasar Court S.
Lakeland, MN 55043

Dear Ted,

It is with great regret that we seem to have no choice but to end our working relationship by taking your home off the market.

As you know, I could have sold this home several times right from the beginning, but due to the unsettled issues within the Association it turned everyone away. To top it off, every time a potential buyer came through the neighborhood, Mr. Swenson would bad-mouth the entire community. It became virtually impossible to sell your home, which is a shame as it is an incredibly comfortable, gorgeous place in an awesome setting.

I'll always be grateful for the friendship we've developed, but am very disappointed that I was unable to help you with the sale of your home.

Warm Regards,

Candace Dahl
Realtor—Coldwell Banker Burnet

Edwards Brothers,Inc!
Thorofare, NJ 08086
28 May, 2010
BA2010148